Hildr

C000186615

What About My Tomorrow?

Today is the
moment you have,
tomorrow is in
God's hands

10/6/17

By

Regina Jele-Ncube

Dedicated to:

Nonkanyiso Kwandokuhle
– my beloved daughter

When you are blessed with your own children you love them unconditionally; yes, even when they mess up they still need you. Work hard and aim high. Never compete with the world but compete with your own self. Be the best that you can be. 'Nonks', you are the most beautiful young woman both inside and out. Be true to who you are and let God be your guide. Learn from my mistakes and be wise. I love you. 'Kino kamama'.

Kennedy Mayibongwe
– my beloved son

I know that one of the yardsticks by which you will measure your success in life is to have been able to raise a happy, stable family. It is a noble thing to aim for, Son, and I am proud it is one of your goals. This is the true mark of a man, not just any man but a God-fearing man. The greatest gift you can ever give to your children is to love and respect their mother with your whole being. Let your speech ooze love. Be a man of your word. Seek wisdom. Continue in your gentle nature. Thank you for being the son that every mother wishes for. I love you, Son. Remember, the suit does not make the man, the man makes the suit!

Contents

What About My Tomorrow?

The Journey Commences

The lump in my throat prevents me from speaking. It feels as though a big hand has been pushed down my throat, denying me much-needed oxygen. My facial expressions are laid bare; the pain, guilt and fear are so obvious; I do a lousy job of hiding it. All they know is that Mum is leaving for another country, for their own good. How much of that they understand is anybody's guess. If I linger a moment longer, trust me, I will say, 'To hell with it all,' get my suitcase out, and turn back.

Life is being so unfair and cruel. Why on earth am I being made to choose between my children and survival? These children are my world, and why is that such a hard concept? Well, the very existence of life itself is threatened.

'No mother should have to go through this,' I whisper to my friend, trying to swallow the tears and snot that are welling up in my mouth. I try in vain to hide my distress. 'They cannot see me crying, Josh,' I say, as I wipe yet another flow of tears.

The goodbyes have no intimacy, instead they are heartbreaking; full of raw, bleeding emotions. The intimate words have fleetingly been shared in the run up to my departure, while attempting to prepare them of my imminent journey to worlds unknown. Even now, when I visit that moment in my book of engraved memories, I can still feel the lump in my throat as though it were yesterday.

Separation is such a cruel thing and whoever said time heals should have a rethink.

'Come on now, get into the car,' Josh says. I wave once more and gaze at them for what might be the very last time. Kennedy looks at me and starts to cry. Nonks opens her big, beautiful eyes in a state of confusion but shows no emotion. That alone rips me inside. People have sacrificed so much for this journey; I dare not change my mind.

I am doing this for them. Right now I'm not sure if I'm just comforting myself by lying or if I'm being real. The funny thing is, the thought keeps me going and makes me more determined.

The plane is full of what look like optimistic, sophisticated travellers, who on first impressions appear sure of both their future and destiny. I sit next to a young lady who is excited to be flying to the UK. We strike up a conversation; luckily we both speak the same language and can also converse in English. She asks if she can sit next to the window – exactly what my seven-year-old daughter would have asked on a journey. This girl is like an excited little child. Without saying a word, I stand up from my seat, let her sit next to the window, and think, *You won't see much of anything really, love.*

'My name is Thandiwe,' she says.

'I'm Regina,' I give my response. If the truth be told she's a bit annoying. I want to sit and be quiet, but I guess being young and without many qualifications from the University of Life she cannot read my mind; neither can she guess how I'm feeling right now. It is a relief to watch her at Heathrow Airport, picking up her luggage after we landed.

People are going this way and that way. It looks so chaotic it makes my head spin. There all sorts of people; it's as if the whole world has converged at

Heathrow. I claim my own suitcase, and head outside. My heart is heavy. I am now in another continent, countless miles away from home. I feel defeated, rejected and scared.

I walk through a large holding area and am greeted by long, snaking queues of people. I look at them, acknowledge them, and nobody acknowledges me. What strikes me is the lack of happy faces. Nobody is smiling or appears to acknowledge another. People just grimace. This must be a true reflection of a dog-eat-dog situation.

I stand in front of an immigration officer. I can't work him out. His face doesn't say much. I'm not sure if he's one of the mean ones or a true specimen of a kind Englishman, and I say a silent prayer to find favour with this man. I smile at him and wait for his response. He takes my paperwork and asks very difficult and sensitive questions. Some of them almost reduce me to tears. This is no time to be tearful and sobbing in front of an English gentleman. I have to hold it together, I have to be strong.

I had sat in my homeland on a daily basis and watched the news. Many of my fellow Zimbabweans had been denied entry when they sought sanctuary in the UK. So, Reader, to be allowed into this country of refuge is an indescribable blessing of blessings. What have I done to deserve such kindness?

Finding my way out of the airport proves a big challenge. I seem to be going in opposite directions. I am following all the other travellers, but for the life of me I can't find my way out. I can read directions and work out signs, so why can't I get out? It takes me a good two hours to exit Heathrow Airport. Out of the airport; hurray!

Oh no, it's not a 'hurray' moment. No one is there to meet or greet me. Friends are busy doing what they have to do to survive in this country. I have only been told to get

3

a bus to Luton. Fair enough, I will do that.

It's pitch dark outside, but it's only the afternoon. That puzzles me and sends me into a further state of disarray.

'Excuse me, what is the time?' I ask a total stranger.

'Three forty-five,' he answers.

'Thank you so much.' I appreciate the stranger's kindness. Now let's clarify something here, Reader; I have done geography at O level and have passed it with a B. I try to remember or recall learning about different time zones and all that jargon. I come to the conclusion those topics must have been taught on the days I played truant. *It's dark and yet it's in the afternoon; get over it, Regina, and find this bus to Luton.*

The Heathrow Airport experience was a traumatic one. I didn't realise how traumatic until I was about to go on a short weekend break away to Germany for my birthday, twelve years later. I began to panic at the thought of being at an airport again. *How will I manage, what questions will I be asked?* Questions came flooding from all over. It was the first time I had flown since 2001. I concluded that I felt this way because I have come to associate airports and flying with separation from loved ones.

Such is life. Count yourself blessed if you have the freedom to globetrot. What is normal to you, is definitely a luxury for the sister next to you. Before you look down on her I urge you to think deeply, count your blessings, and spare her a thought.

4

Family Life

Unless the Lord build the house, the builders labour in vain. Unless the Lord watches over the city, the guards stand watch in vain. (NIV)
Psalms 127 vs 1-2

I have a brilliant, strong mother. She is my hero. I can never find words to describe her. She does not believe in idle hands and an idle mind. She is a very wise and intelligent woman. I am not saying she is perfect but she has taught me life's greatest lessons. Lessons that no academic textbooks can relay, lessons no professor can deliver from a podium. I will cherish these lessons to the day I draw my last breath.

Even though not academic herself, she strongly believes in educating her children. She will move heaven and earth to ensure her children get an education. She not only believes in academic education; she believes you can learn from all around you. And she makes me learn, sometimes the hard way. She works hard to supplement the family income and support my dad in providing for us. There is just something about a mother and daughter relationship. It is a very special one.

Our home is a two-bedroomed house. I have two older brothers and for a long while I am the baby of the family until my little sister decides to take away my crown and depose me from my eight-year reign. Life is fun. We play a lot, and we squabble equally as much.

Mama is the disciplinarian in the house. She teaches us how to behave in private and in public. She teaches self-respect, respect for others, and respect for property and everything around us. She teaches us morals and standards. Labour is distributed equally, regardless of your gender. She believes he who has a mouth to eat, should know how to cook and clean.

I am mischievous and I get into trouble. I misbehave at school and get conks on my head all the time. The benefits of working hard are instilled as early as I can remember. As an adult, I now thrive on work and if Mama had not worked on me I would be one lazy, carefree person who walks around thinking society and the world owes me a living. How can I not be grateful to such parents?

We live in town and yet Mum and Dad have a piece of land that we till and tender, and on which we grow maize. As far as I am concerned this is a farm, a proper field and not just a piece of land. How I hate having to be up at the crack of dawn and being given an everlasting list. I call it food for work. One dares not fool around: do your chores and you are in Mama's good books. No work, no food, even if you think you should be entitled. You will get it when the list for the day is all ticked off.

The best days of my life are my school days, especially my secondary school days. I attend a girls-only boarding school, an Anglican Mission School. These days are full of indescribable fun. Learning is both hard and fun. Hard because there is so much to learn and comprehend. Fun because I'm away from 'Nagging Mother Dearest' for at least eight or nine months a year. Fun because I get into trouble, homework is sometimes not handed in on time, we're making noise after lights-out, and simply being downright rude without realising. You see, I haven't

always been as snow white 'as some would like to believe. Life would have been so boring if I had been a Miss Goody Two Shoes! Sometimes I look back and wish I had never grown up. Unfortunately, life has to happen.

Family Under Siege

God is our refuge and strength, an ever present help in trouble.
Psalms 46 vs 1

I am nearing the end of my primary schooling. Something is in the air; there is uneasiness in the country. The Liberation War is raging, the Rhodesian Army is wreaking havoc on the natives and so is the Liberation Army. People want their freedom and not this stupid Zimbabwe-Rhodesia nonsense between Ian Smith and Abel Muzorewa. I don't understand much but, trust me, I see and hear a lot, and some of the whisperings catch my attention.

The year is 1979, I cannot remember the date but I know it is a Friday night. My dad has been working away from home for a week and we are expecting him back this particular Friday. We wait for Dad to walk through the door any time soon. The sun has set and Dad is a no-show. We try to resist, but Mum has none of it: it's bedtime and we have to go to bed. I guess my solace is that when I wake up the following morning, Dad will be home.

The next thing I remember, Mama is trying to wake us up. She seems to be in a panic, and with eyes half-closed I can see she is holding my little sister in her arms. She is shaking us frantically, but we are in a deep sleep. She shakes my brothers and shouts out our names. Now we jump out of that slumber. That shout is definitely one not to be ignored.

'Wake up, wake up!' She is trying to help us get ourselves together. She is saying something which I don't understand. There is a loud banging noise coming from outside. She whispers to us not to be afraid. That alone scares us. Our bedroom door is ajar and I catch a glimpse of my dad amidst all the confusion. As we attempt to get ourselves decent, there is a sudden deafening noise. It is the sound of gunshots. We all freeze. There is more shouting and pounding on our front door, I'm positive that door will fall off its hinges any minute soon. I feel like I'm in a Chuck Norris movie set. Whatever's going on, I know we are in danger.

'You are under siege, open the door and come out now! If you try anything you will all be shot,' a voice roars from outside the door, sending untold fear into all of us. A tool or some equipment is definitely being used to bang on our front door. Nowhere on God's earth will I ever forget that voice. We live in a block of flats and ours is on the top floor.

Dad finds the door keys and unlocks the door An army of soldiers is waiting. Am I dreaming or is this for real? My cousin-sister doesn't even have time to put on a dress. She went to bed in her knickers the previous night, and in the ensuing confusion there is no time to find a dress or something decent. Right now her modesty is not of the essence, but only staying alive.

We go out the door in single file. Dad is in front; Mum is behind him, carrying my baby sister on her back. She is ordered to carry her in her arms. My cousin-sister and I follow behind Mum, and my brothers are at the back.

'Put your hands up, or I will shoot!' one soldier bellows out.

'Come down slowly!' shouts yet another. We march down the stairs, one after the other, and as we land on the last step we are greeted by more heavily armed soldiers. We are violently strip-searched and when they are satisfied we are harmless we are forced to sit down. The ground is drenched as it has just rained – we're right in the middle of the rainy season. It appears there is a whole barracks of soldiers outside. It is then that we realise our lives hang in the balance. The most confusing part is that we don't know why.

After about half an hour Dad is ordered back into the house.

Our flat is ransacked. It's as though a hurricane has hit it. It is turned upside down and inside out. While my dad is being quizzed inside, the rest of the family is still outside under a heavily armed guard. All I see are white soldiers. Most of them have an Afrikaans accent. They are fairly big in stature and very hairy. During the liberation struggle in Rhodesia, white South African Boers were drafted into the Army to come and fight the 'terrorists', hence these soldiers at our home tonight. There are only two black soldiers that I can see. One of them is ordered into the house, by one of his commanders I presume. It transpires that during the search they came across a Seventh Day Adventist hymnal in my native language. There is such a fuss and concern over the hymnal, and I am later told they suspect it's a collection of liberation songs. I also learn one soldier comes to our rescue and verifies it's a Christian song book.

After what seems like an eternity, Dad is finally allowed to come outside and join us. The soldiers that are inside the flat come down carrying a suitcase. We are ordered back inside. We are still none the wiser as to why this is happening.

My dad and two older brothers are taken away by the soldiers. Now during that era, if an individual was taken away under such circumstances it meant one thing: they were never coming back to you alive. If you received their body to bury, that would be a welcome blessing.

I had known we were in danger earlier on, but when my dad and my two brothers get inside that vehicle, then I know without question it is the end. We watch helplessly as they are forced into the horrible police car. I take one look at my mama, and her face says it all. This is definitely the last we will ever see of them. She is already bereaved. She is helpless and is in despair. I feel her pain. These are the three most important men in my life and they are being taken away. They are my heroes and I want them with me. I want to play with my brothers and I want Dad to come and tickle me again. I whisper a prayer. 'God, I want Daddy, Shacky and Gree back home.'

We are back inside our flat, only it looks nothing like the place I have called home all my life. The scene is indescribable. Clothes, photos, everything is strewn across the floor. Our blankets are not in sight.

Mama clears a space, digs through the rubble, and pulls out some blankets so we can sleep. It must be around 2:30 in the morning. Even though I am a child, there is no way I am falling asleep. I am trying to make sense of the events of the last two hours or so. We huddle together and gaze into space.

At the first light of dawn, Mum goes into the kitchen and makes some porridge. We stare at our plates and cannot bring ourselves to eat. We appear to be grieving. When Mum is not looking I peep through the windows, hoping the emerging morning might have answers for me. We long for another human presence; we need human contact other than ourselves. We yearn for somebody to turn up and put things into perspective.

The morning is unusually calm today, which in itself is not normal. A usual Saturday morning in my neighbourhood is abuzz with life. It's as though time has stood still and all has gone into hibernation. Had my brothers been around, we would be getting ready to go to church, squabbling about how long I have been in the bathroom, or they would have been telling me to stop straightening my hair and get a move on. My hair straighteners at the time – a smooth, round stone that would go on top of Mama's cooker – get heated and then straight on to my head to straighten my hair. How I didn't get burnt, I would never know. It was the beauty secret of many a teenager in my time.

This is a different morning. Firstly, I am not getting ready for church as would have been the case, my brothers and my dad are not around and the neighbourhood is extremely calm. There is no human activity taking place. We yearn for some form of human contact, and none is forthcoming. How can we be so lonely in a neighbourhood that is usually active, and bursting with people? The thirst for that human contact is so severe we are almost gulping. We need the human touch; where is everybody when we need them? Nothing makes sense. We want our neighbours to come and look out for us: after all, we know they are a lovely bunch.

The first human contact we get is around eleven in the morning. We are sitting outside under a peach tree. The flat is uninhabitable after last night's events; a bit of fresh air might bring a little perspective. A neighbour comes over, and before long a group is gathered around us.

We learn that the gunshots we had heard had been aimed at my dad who had been making his way to the bathroom, unaware of the looming trouble. The balcony has a wall that leaves one's top half exposed on the walk through to the bathroom. Unbeknown to my dad his house was the target of an Army raid and therefore any movement meant the soldiers could open fire indiscriminately. That wall saved my dad as the bullets missed him and hit the wall instead. I can still picture those bullet marks to this day.

It is fascinating to little me, to hear our neighbours tell Mum their version of last night's events. They tell us there were more police and soldiers surrounding the entire block of flats. Theories start emerging as to why this event took place. No one can validate them. The truth is, nobody knows.

One of the neighbours asks Mama about my dad and brothers. Mama enlightens them. The neighbours' reactions say it all. They don't need to say a word; everybody pretty much knows the expected outcome. We just sit and wait, Mum says something to the effect of, 'If they only bring back the bodies for me to bury.' We sit and wait.

It's after 2 p.m., and a police car pulls up outside. We steel ourselves for the most dreaded news. A white policeman comes out, and after a few seconds another door opens, and there are my dad and my brothers. The urge to run towards them is so overwhelming. You see, Reader, this is one of those moments in life to breathe a painful sigh of relief.

I take one hard look at the policeman that escorts them and decide to stay put. My dad is carrying the suitcase that had been confiscated. There isn't much communication going on. The police turn round and go back to their car. It's only then we embrace and kiss those that have come back from the dead. Reader, I hope you truly connect with my last statement here. To have your loved ones come back to you alive during that era was a miracle of blessings.

The suitcase of interest belongs to an uncle who is working in South Africa. It is later revealed that as a family we had been suspected of harbouring a terrorist in recent months and that the suitcase must have belonged to the so-called terrorist. Such is life under British colonial rule. As black people we are constantly under surveillance and suspected of all sorts.

More light is shed later on. My parents are told an anonymous call was made which informed the authorities we had entertained a 'fugitive and terrorist'. Upon making their investigations it is clear that they meant my uncle, who had visited us from South Africa a month prior to this incident and there is the possibility that the caller either had genuine concerns or just wanted to get us into trouble. Those that are fighting for an independent Zimbabwe are branded terrorists. As a black person you are Government Enemy Number One. For now, let's just say I am over the moon my dad and brothers are back in one piece.

Why Him And Not Me?

Take my yoke upon you and learn from me, for I am gentle and humble in heart, and will find rest for your souls.
Matthew 11 vs 29

A few months go by. Events of that Friday night are slowly being laid into my memory box. We get on with our lives as normally as we can. When I am asleep I think I can hear distant noises. I don't think much about it. Morning soon breaks, it's time to get ready for school. It turns out the noise I thought I heard was real. It was the sound of guns.

I'm not clear what has happened exactly. Rumours start doing the rounds. 'A family has been wiped out in a raid,' people say. I make my way to school and meet up with other schoolchildren on the way. The event of the day is on our lips. It turns out the house that has been raided is the home of one of my classmates. I am curious and want to see for myself. So I make a detour and go to the scene; after all, everyone is headed that way.

I am welcomed by the smell of fresh blood, and death is in the air. I take a look from a distance and I can see walls covered in blood. I dare not get any closer as the place is still heavily guarded. You might wonder why we are even allowed in such close proximity to the horrible scene; I guess it is to prove to us they can do to us what they have just done to this family if we dare cross the line. Suddenly

I am taken back to that Friday when my home was also raided.

This could have been my house, and that could have been my blood. I run away from the scene, tears flowing.

I take my seat in class and one of us is missing. We all look confused and so is our teacher. The thoughts come back again: that empty seat could have been mine. I feel guilty to be alive and I cannot share that guilt with anyone. I know people will tell me I am only a child and ask what I have to be guilty about, but unfortunately I feel it. I am aware life has to go on in spite of one of us missing from class today. The sad reality is he is not just playing truant, he is dead. Right now I just need peace within my soul. This is too much for me to comprehend.

Run For The Hills

*I lift up my eyes to the hills – where does my help come
from? My help comes from the Lord, the maker of heaven
and earth. He will not let your foot slip – he who watches
over you will not slumber: indeed, he who watches over
Israel will neither slumber nor sleep.*
Psalms 121 vs 1-4

It is March 1980, and people have voted for the first time
for a free Zimbabwe. The Liberation War has been fought.
Personally, one thing I look forward to is having the
freedom to attend any school of choice. Rhodesia has a
two-tier school system: top-notch schools, a preserve of
the white children, are referred to as Group A schools, and
ours are referred to as Group B schools. The distinction is
clear. The 'A' buildings are state of the art. The pupils are
offered sports like tennis, rugby and golf, whilst we are
made to play football and, my gosh, don't we try our best.
I'm sure you understand why that is top priority to little
me.

Lives have been sacrificed. Mothers have lost their
children so we can have a free Zimbabwe. May their souls
rest in peace, and shame on us lest we forget. The masses
have said a firm 'No' to continued British colonial rule.
The two main parties are the Zimbabwe African National
Union (ZANU, led by Robert Gabriel Mugabe) and the
Zimbabwe African Patriotic Union (ZAPU, led by the late

Joshua Mgqabuko Nkomo). The results are out and the shoots of tribal divisions are rearing their ugly heads.

The first signs of the divide within the country are evident. I am still a bit young and naive to understand what is happening but I can see things are not OK.

I witness and eavesdrop at 'big people's' conversations at any given chance. It would appear they all believe there has been a rigging of votes. Something about the Lancaster House agreement; it's a bit too complicated for me to understand. They appear to have compelling and moving arguments that Joshua Mgqabuko Nkomo should have won the elections instead of Mugabe. This is confusing to little me and at the time the debate is boring. I leave them to it and go and play hopscotch with my friends.

Now I am aware there are two main political parties fighting against colonial rule and there are two main armed forces to be integrated into the national army: ZIPRA led by Mgqabuko and ZANLA led by Mugabe. I have an uncle who actually joined the liberation struggle. Thank God he came back alive. The integration of the two forces is underway and they are stationed at different bases throughout the country. Two of the bases are in a township called Entumbane in Bulawayo. We are happy to have our 'boys' back. They teach people new liberation songs and people love it.

I remember this particular morning, there was one of those exhilarating moments when the boys marched round the neighbourhood singing those catchy liberation songs. Before I knew it I was part of the crowd. I was so taken in the heat of the moment I did not realise how far I had moved from home. Now this is a normal school day and I should really be getting ready for school. I finally make my way back home, and I am comforted by the fact that there are some of my friends in the group. When I get home,

Mum is waiting for me. Let's just say I am grateful to have lived to tell the tale.

One beautiful Sunday afternoon in November 1980, I am throwing one stinking strop because I have not been allowed to go with my brother to a football match. Mama says, 'You are not going, young lady, stick your head in them books.' My face is like thunder, and nobody is paying me any attention and my feelings amount to nothing. Mama gives me 'the look' and I know it's time to fix up or face the music. I fix up immediately. I know only too well the meaning of that look. After pretending to read, I play with my little sister. She is annoying me a wee bit, so I go back to memorising my times tables.

It is around six in the evening and there seems to be a commotion outside, but I cannot figure it out. All I hear is the elders saying, '*Sekuliwa Entumbane, abafana sebebulalana.*' (Trouble at Entumbane, the boys are killing each other). In no time the whole neighbourhood gathers together.

Breaking News!

Suddenly there are sounds, unmistakably they are gunshots, heavy gunfire. How can I mistake gunshots? Panic sets in. My brother would have to make his way back home from the football game; somehow, the trouble is between him and home. This is a big worry for us. We stay put and the sound of guns gets worse by the minute. This is becoming a full blown war. It is now getting dark outside and still there is no sign of my brother.

A decision has to be made whether we take cover inside the house or we flee. We constantly sneak and peep to try and assess the danger. A decision is made; we have to run for the hills as it is no longer safe to remain indoors and within close proximity of the boiling point. The sound of gunshots is getting closer and closer. Mama urges us to dress appropriately for the flight.

We leave in haste. The whole neighbourhood leaves together. We head for the outskirts. A place called Hyde Park is decided to be a place of safety. It's around the rainy season again. It is wet and there are loads of creepy creatures. We walk for what appears to be an eternity. Even as we walk we can still hear the gunshots.

Finally, we find some plain greenery heavily vegetated and we make ourselves comfortable. Some of us children try and fall asleep at some point. We are awakened by the arrival of another group also seeking refuge. There are whispers among the parents; I am too sleepy to eavesdrop this time.

The sound of guns is dying down. We are woken up and told it's time to make a move back. Nobody questions the wisdom of that decision. We are quiet as we walk back home. It's scarier walking back than it was heading for the hills. Our feet are heavy, our bodies and minds are all over the place. Most of us children are half asleep and we are rebuked and told to be alert.

Three quarters of the way back home, we spot a lone soldier. He is fully armed. Now there is a dilemma here. Who is this soldier, which of the forces does he belong to, and which language should we use to speak to him? Important to know, seeing as our survival at this point rests with this one soldier. He sees us, aims his gun to our direction and keeps approaching. We come to a standstill. He moves closer and orders us to put our hands up.

'*Bwanji, bamboo,*' (translated: How are you, sir?) This is one of the native languages from Zambia. My dad is Zambian and has always taken pride in his mother tongue despite residing in Zimbabwe his entire life. The lone soldier responds in siNdebele and dad answers him back in siNdebele. You can see all the older people breathing a sigh of relief and they start a conversation with the soldier. He does not give much away despite being probed. He assures them he will get us home safely.

In my little mind I'm thinking, 'You are just one body, how can you protect us?' Anyway we walk on by and follow his instructions. He makes sure each family gets into their home and he disappears as more gun sounds fill the air. My brother is still not home. He stayed at my grandma's house till it was safe to return.

Months later I ask Mum and Dad why Dad chose to speak to the lone soldier in his Zambian native language. The explanation I'm given is fascinating. If the lone soldier had been from the ZANLA forces and dad spoke in siNdebele, he might have assumed we were supporters of ZIPRA, and had Dad spoken in Shona and the soldier was from the ZIPRA, the opposite assumption would have led to our demise.

This war is the manifestation of the bitter hatred and rivalry between the siNdebele and Shona speaking people of Zimbabwe. What a sad state for society to fall so low. The two tribes that stood shoulder to shoulder fighting the common enemy are now at war with each other. All of a sudden people appear to have forgotten the lives lost during the Liberation War; tribe and language appear to take centre stage. What does the enemy we just fought think of us? He is laughing at us with scorn.

Tribalism and its divides: one of society's worst enemies. It breeds deep-seated, unfounded hatred among people. How can we forget Rwanda and many other unfortunate senseless losses of life? Let the recorded facts of history always serve as a reminder, and I only wish history's mistakes are never repeated, for the sakes of our children and generations to come.

The unrest spreads to other parts of the country. I hear about fierce fighting again between the two forces at a place called Silalabuhwa, which goes on for days. Parts of the country come to a standstill. I miss some days of school as it is just not safe to be away from home. I am annoyed at this. You see, Reader, I prefer to be at school rather than being home. Staying at home means, clean your bedroom, complete this chore and that chore, and it's just not cool. You would have thought with the unrest in the country, Mum would have cut us some slack, but she makes sure we do what we have to do.

So many theories come up as these disturbances continue, one of them being that ZIPRA forces feel they are being marginalised and not being fairly grafted into the newly forming national army. I don't know what the truth is and it's a bit too much and too political for little me to comprehend. From my constant questioning, Mum gives me my first serious political lesson.

'You see, Regi, politics is a dirty game,' she says. 'You can't always trust what you see, hear or what you are told. Politicians play enemies during the day and they are friends during the night when the world is not looking on. A politician will invite you over for tea while planning your execution, what I'm saying is all politicians care about nobody else but themselves.' I did not understand 95 per cent of it at the time, but as the years have gone by, it all makes sense.

It takes Joshua Nkomo to fly down to these areas and talk to the 'boys' and broker a truce between the two forces. I remember seeing a low flying helicopter and hearing a very commanding, fatherly voice, '*Bekani izikhali phansi bafana. Ukubambana bafana.*' (Put down your weapons and unite). Talk of living up to his title as the father of the nation. He is affectionately known as 'Father Zimbabwe'. The boys listen and there is a temporary ceasefire. I am using the term ceasefire very loosely here.

Boarding School Life

The fear of the Lord is the beginning of wisdom, and knowledge of the Holy One is understanding.
Proverbs 9 vs 10

Years roll on. I am progressing and becoming more politically aware and up to date to a certain degree with issues surrounding the governance of my country. There appears to be more focus on party politics rather than a national emphasis. I am seeing a thread of party symbols rather than symbols of a united country. Most of the national celebrations do not encompass all those represented in Zimbabwe. Slowly but surely, all high-flying posts are filled up by people from one tribe more than the other. People are not getting jobs on their own merits and based on their qualifications. Talk of being born on to the right and wrong side. There is such a felt presence of 'them' as never before.

Maybe it is fair to say I am becoming more aware there is a tribe other than my own. All official bodies assume you are a Shona-speaking person, and in most instances you are expected to answer in Shona regardless of whether you know the language. Some of us had to learn the language in order to survive. It is a common belief amongst siNdebele people that Shona-speaking people have never felt the need to learn our language, and that we have always accommodated them. This could be a far-fetched theory. Let's learn to live together, people, for goodness sake, please. We only have one life to live.

One theory that most people have come to believe is this: there could be six people in the room, five speaking siNdebele and one Shona-speaking, yet the tendency is that the five Ndebele speakers will automatically try and speak Shona to accommodate that one person. That to me is patriotism, but it changes its dynamics if you are compelled. Thank goodness I have another language up my sleeve, at least that is how I look at it.

I am a little grown now. I have secured a secondary place in one of the best boarding schools. Not that I know any different, but my parents think this school will give me a good chance in life. It is a girls-only school in Nyamandlovu, and has recently reopened after closure during the war.

The prospect of being away from home for certain periods of time is both exciting and scary, but I quickly settle in. It's a whole new world and it's not bad, actually. I make friends and get on with it. The best time is the weekend meal. We get freshly baked bread once a week on a Sunday after mass. St James is an Anglican school, so attending mass is a must. Most teachers are white and there are a fair few nuns who also teach.

We are allowed to dress up on Saturdays. The number of 'going out dresses' is limited to only three. Slowly I realise the seniors don't adhere to this rule; they have actually brought a trunkload of clothes. So, I tell myself, next term, I'm also bringing more clothes, but there is one person to go through, Mama, and I know she will be hard to penetrate and convince. I am determined to try, though. Before I know it, my first year in secondary school is over and boarding life has been great.

1982, and I'm now in my second year at secondary

school. We hear of another fight between the two forces in Entumbane. We worry over our parents. We don't know if they are OK. It is before the era of mobiles, we cannot communicate with them; we just pray and hope they are fine. The worry is evident, so much so that the school principal addresses us in an effort to calm and reassure us. Weeks after, the majority of us start receiving letters from home informing us not to worry they are OK, whatever OK means. We get snippets of newspapers from our teachers and we read and comprehend what we can.

Wednesday afternoon, I'm lucky enough to lay my hands on a newspaper. A headline catches my attention: DUMISO DABENGWA AND LOOKOUT MASUKU ARRESTED. I am developing my interest in politics. A teacher, seeing my interest explains more. I understand to a certain degree and that is good enough. Now these two men who appear to have been arrested are two of the many stalwarts within the ZIPRA army and, trust me, this is not good at all. I can sense more trouble on the way.

We no longer feel safe being at a boarding school. We learn of a new army called the Gugurahundi being drafted into parts of Matabeleland. I later learn this army was specially trained by the North Koreans following a treaty or agreement between Mugabe and the then North Korean leader, although do not know for sure if this is true. They are also referred to as the 5th Brigade. They are distinguished by their red berets.

Unarmed civilians are being indiscriminately killed around the regions of Matabeleland, and my school is around one of the target areas. As if that is not enough, another word is added to our vocabulary. We learn there is also another army or group of people called dissidents. Some say they are disgruntled ZIPRA forces, others say it's disgruntled siNdebele people who are not happy that Mugabe is in power.

There is panic amongst our parents and some start to remove their children from the school. Some of us stay put with the prayers from our parents that we don't come to any harm. The country disintegrates into more chaos. Some of the stories we hear of the killings are too horrific to believe. The world looks on and I'm not sure what it is doing to help.

In March 1983, there is sadder, horrible news. The 5th Brigade has killed fifty five young men and women on the banks of Cewale River in Lupane. I pray to God that this is not true, but unfortunately it is. It is reported that they force-marched sixty two in total, and seven survive but are wounded. I don't know what to make of this headline. One thing is for sure I feel the loss of the region. The atrocities carried out are beyond comprehension. A demonic spirit has been unleashed and it would appear there is no exorcising it.

It is estimated that in total the 5th Brigade killed around twenty thousand civilians in Matabeleland during that time. What a loss of life.

In my quest to become well informed, I speak to a well-read, elderly man who explains that the term Gugurahundi is 'the early rain which washes away the chaff before spring rains'. How tragic that the government, a government that should have been protecting its people and heritage, now views some of its people as chaff. How low can humanity sink?

Being at school is not that much fun anymore. We are scared we could be the subject of sexual violence. Women and children have suffered untold pain during the war, and we pray nothing happens to those of us who are still pupils at this school. Thank God we don't come to any such harm but find ourselves with an imposed curfew.

We are under scrutiny and constant surveillance from

the soldiers who have set up camp around the school. We can no longer attend evening studies as part of the curfew. We cannot be seen outside the school dormitories or school grounds after 7 p.m. It feels weird having soldiers around the school. Some try to be too familiar with us and are immediately confronted by a very dedicated, fearless principal. God rest her soul. Mrs Beadall is prepared to die for her girls. Each time she thinks the soldiers are up to no good she confronts them straight away. This makes her Enemy Number One.

On this one occasion, she has been summoned to the local police station. The signs are not good; our principal might not come back to us. We hold a prayer vigil for her. She has refused to allow the soldiers to move their 'temporary' camp any nearer than they already are. The unrest is so brutal anyone who dares oppose the government disappears. This seems like we are back in the Rhodesia era, only we are in a free Zimbabwe.

This era has never really left most of the people of the Matabeleland and sadly enough some still bear the physical and emotional scars.

I sincerely pray that those people of Matabeleland can find it in their hearts to forgive and move on for their own sakes and for generations to come, and that the generations to come will learn from history and avoid its mistakes. Maybe a dedicated truth and reconciliation drive would have helped to heal and forge a true forgiveness.

Stranger On The Bus

'There are no coincidences in life. What person that wandered in and out of your life was there for some purpose, even if they caused you harm. Sometimes, it doesn't make sense the short periods of time we get with people, or the outcomes from their choices. However, if you turn it over to God he promises that you will see the big picture in the hereafter. Nothing is too small to be a mistake.'
Shannon L. Alder

Boarding school is not always fun and games. Being on holiday is heaven sent. Now I prefer and look forward to being home more than being at school. I appreciate Mama's hard work and you know I have learnt a thing or two about managing my time.

The last day of term is such fun and we hardly sleep, and yet that seems the longest night of the entire term. We are constantly checking the time every hour on the hour. The highlight of the last day is the school assembly. The church is abuzz with noise and giggly, excited girls, and when it comes to singing we give it a real belter. 'Lord dismiss us with thy blessing' is *the* song. We don't care if we lose our voices, we are glad to be going home and being dismissed from a 'convent'. The nuns are too strict with us, and we are happy for little droppings of freedom. As we come out of assembly, the coaches are lined up and soon we will be boarding and going home. We sing throughout the entire journey, and by the time some of us get to our parents we *have* lost our voices.

I am on my school holiday after the first term of 1983. I have visited my aunt for a couple of days. You see, extended family is part of my culture and aunties have to be visited whether you like it or not. I travel on the bus back home after my visit. There are a few spaces left in the bus. I find one next to a good-looking guy. As I sit down he shuffles as though to make me comfortable sitting next to him. 'Thank you,' I acknowledge his kind gesture.

'It's such a hot day today,' he says to me.

'Yeah, it is,' I answer him. Silence for most of the journey. Good, after all Mum taught me not to talk to strangers!

'Where are you coming from?' he speaks again.

Gosh he is a nosy one.

'From visiting my aunt,' I decide to answer.

'My name is Alfred,' he volunteers. I know he is expecting me to tell him mine. I don't, at least for now. That you see, is my prerogative.

'You have not told me your name,' he speaks again.

He is beginning to get on my nerves. *He is just a guy on the bus, why should I tell him my name?*

'It's not really important for you to know my name.' I think of that moment now and laugh at the way I displayed childish behaviour. Well, it felt good at the time.

'That's OK, you do not have to tell me your name if you don't want,' he answers very calmly.

Damn right I don't. After a while I tell him my second name. 'My name is Amanda.'

'That a beautiful name,' he responds.

'Thanks,' I say, rather dismissively.

I am two stops away from getting off, so out of politeness

I tell the stranger that I will be getting off the bus. Coincidentally, he is also getting off at the same bus stop and seems to be headed in the same direction. We have some small talk, and I rush off to get home. 'I'm home now, thanks once again,' I find myself saying, but I'm not sure what I am thanking him for.

The days roll on by and before I know it, it's the weekend again. I'm chatting away to my sisters on our way back to a church youth meeting, when suddenly a voice calls out my name.

'Hi, Amanda.' The voice comes from behind us. I am startled: nobody in my neighbourhood knows my second name. I turn round and who do I see but the stranger from the bus?

'Hi,' I respond. *Why is this man in the vicinity? I have forgotten his name, and he picks that up immediately.*

'You have forgotten my name,' he says as he smiles at me. I want to come up with a lie but decide against it and face the truth.

'I guess I have,' I admit.

'It's Alfred,' he reminds me.

The rest of my school holiday he seems to be lurking around my neighbourhood. We chat about this and that. I'm scared to be seen with him: firstly I hardly know him and secondly this is an era when you cannot be seen with a guy next to you for no apparent reason. Should that happen, trust me, you will be dead meat. How times have changed and moved on.

We talk a lot and vaguely get to know each other. I establish he has feelings for me, whatever that means. Weeks before the holiday is over it would appear we think we are an item. Yep, we are doing the girlfriend and boyfriend thing in our heads.

Play Hard, Study Hard

All work and no play makes Jack a dull boy
Common proverb

Two winks and the school holiday is over. Tomorrow it's back to the 'convent' as we refer to it. I am dying to tell my friends of the stranger on the bus. I know I will be the envy of those coming back to school with no boyfriend story. You see, being in a girls-only school, that lack of male attention does play on our minds, and when we get that attention we feel a million dollars. Having a boyfriend entitles you to join the elite group at school, at least that is what we think. You think you are more beautiful than the rest of them, you think you know how to strut your behind. So you see, Reader, I will be moving up a notch in this social setting. Feeling left out, others resort to fake it and tell all these romantic stories of imaginary boyfriends. Others are so convincing they are believed. Such is growing up during my teenage days. No harm is done, it's all part of the bigger world.

We receive our mail in the communal dining room twice a week, Tuesday and Friday evenings. Prefects on duty are responsible for giving it out. In the centre of the dining hall, they place a large trolley with all the letters and parcels from our loved ones. This is one of the highlights of our Tuesday and Friday dinner time. When you are away from home and loved ones, anything to connect you with your nearest and dearest is more than welcome. Letters are the in thing. A letter from Mum and Dad means pocket money. A letter from my brothers means more pocket money. Well, a letter from Alfred means countless I love yous, and that makes a girl feel special.

Regina Amanda Jele. I know who has written that letter even before handling it. That letter is read over and over again or even put under a pillow when I go to bed in the hope the sweet words will aid a blissful sleep. This particular day I receive four letters from him. I am over the moon, and working my behind as I walk to the mail trolley to collect them. My word, do I get stick from the prefects on duty. They demand I read my mail in front of them. I look at them and think, *you must be having a laugh*, for this girl is definitely not one to pick on. I will fight my corner and give as much as I get. In the twenty-first century this amounts to bullying; back then we called it sizing each other up and it taught us to settle our scores.

I have a very special friend. We have been close since we started secondary school. She is intelligent and a very lovely person to be around. She doesn't say a lot but she is pretty smart. There is strong telepathy between the two of us. Her pain is my pain just as her joy is mine and the opposite is true. This bond is special. The friendship we share is very unique and words cannot begin to explain. MaPhi, you are a true gem. Distance physically separates us but in spirit we are one. Thank goodness for modern technology. We are just a finger tap away from each other.

All is not going well at school at this time. Somehow we are not happy. The food is horrible, and the manual labour is just too much. The nuns work us to the bone and they are such a mean bunch of people. There are too many restrictions on us.

A secret meeting is held and it is decided that we should

stage a demonstration. We run wild and refuse to go for classes. The outcome is not what we expected. Some get expelled from school. Now we feel helpless and cannot save the unlucky ones. The blame game ensues. People sell others out to save their own skins. I am one of the few that get a second chance.

Another few winks, I will soon be sitting my O level exams. It is important that I pass. Passing these will definitely set me up in life. I have to study hard and not allow any distractions, and Alfred at the time is a rather costly distraction as far as my education is concerned. I dump him. I write him a letter and tell him we are done and it was nice knowing him and reading his love letters.

Teacher Training

*Wisdom cannot be imparted. Wisdom that a wise man
attempts to impart always sounds like foolishness to
someone else . . . Knowledge can be communicated, but
not wisdom. One can find it, live it, do wonders through
it, but one cannot communicate and teach it.'*
Hermann Hesse, Siddhartha

As soon as my O-level results are out, I head for the
teacher training college to try and secure a place. That has
always been the profession for me. Mama and my brothers
are trying to steer me towards the medical field, but that is
not what I want. The more they persuade, the more I dig
my heels in.

Acquiring a college place is no longer based on one's
merit but on who you know in high places, plus the tribe
and language you belong to, or speak. There is a queue of
aspiring teachers all hoping to get a place at this college. It
is a long queue. I quickly lose any hope of securing a place
but I stay put and hope for the best. There is a bit of
pushing and jostling. All want to secure a place. *If no one
puts this in order, there is going to be a stampede soon.*

Some college authorities come and organise us, but it
doesn't last long. Some want to jump the queue.
Something fishy is going on around the officials
registering the students but I cannot quite put my finger
on it. It would appear as though money is changing hands.

Yes, bribes are definitely the order of the day. I'm standing there thinking if I am asked for a bribe that's it for me. I don't have a penny to my name.

A certain man (who turned out to be one of the lecturers at the college) spots me and comes straight towards me. His face looks very familiar but I cannot place him at all.

'Good afternoon, young lady, can I please see your results? I hand him the envelope. 'Well done you,' he says, before disappearing with my results.

'Wait there,' he says, pointing to a spot away from the queue. I hesitate, I don't want to lose my place in the queue. He senses my hesitation; he repeats himself this time with an authoritative voice. I act swiftly as he disappears behind the reception desk. The next I see of him he is handing me an acceptance letter confirming I have been offered a place at the college. Talk about a miracle! He didn't even give me chance to thank him.

'See you when the programme begins, young lady.'

It transpires the mystery man knows me. He later tells me I go to the same church as his fiancée, and that each time he visits my church he is impressed by my behaviour. *Really, Mr Mhlanga! I don't know what sort of eyesight he has. It's definitely not twenty-twenty vision.* Let's just say he saves the day.

Being the free social butterfly that I am, I quickly make friends at college. I stay there during the week, and go home over the weekends. It's not every weekend of course. Soon the visits home become few and far between. Assignments, group presentations, lectures and critiquing academic papers become the order of the day and I like it.

A level of political awareness is slowly and surely being embedded in my psyche. Soon I realise I have a strong opinion on the systems that govern us. The people of Matabeleland continue to feel marginalised. Even the student ratios at college bear this out. For every siNdebele-speaking student there are three or four Shona-speaking students, despite the college being in Matabeleland. We feel strongly about it. These and other issues create tensions among students and lecturers. It is a very sad state of affairs.

A group of six of us become very close friends. The group consists of three boys and three girls. As a normal student institute people start coupling us up. Some strongly believe we are 'couples'. It's a bit annoying trying to explain that we are just good friends. There is Themba, Nomusa, Ryan, Dave, Chantelle[1] and myself. Chantelle is the niece of the late Joshua Mgqabuko Nkomo. We look out for each other, we play together and study together. Nomusa and I are now both settled in the UK. I am in touch with Themba through Facebook, and I don't know what has become of Ryan, Dave and Chantelle, but I know wherever they are they will have done well for themselves.

A new student union president is needed and we have to vote one in. The vote is political and it bears semblance to the tribal divides. Mind games are at work. The Shona-speaking students have four candidates going for the position. The siNdebele students have one, and we all rally around him, so he wins, and we are happy. College life continues with its challenges.

It's Sunday and I've spent the whole weekend at college. I am looking forward to going to a football match later. The team I support is playing an old rival. This is no ordinary match; it is a big one. Highlanders FC are playing Dynamos FC, there is a lot riding on this match. The two teams are now so politicised it's just unbelievable. Dynamos is a football team with roots associated with

---

[1] All names have been changed

Shona-speaking, and Highlanders has roots associated with siNdebele. Any games between these two are viewed as Nkomo versus Mugabe. Whichever team wins, the supporters feel fiercely opposed. Even the number of police dispatched trebles when these two teams clash. It has become a norm that fist fights will occur either before the game or after the game. It's risky being out and about when these two teams are concerned, but we still venture out.

I am clad in my team colours for this big game. The two team colours are all so visible that day. Everyone is showing and pledging their support. Each prays and keeps their fingers crossed they win the game. This is no ordinary match. It is a cup final, so, Reader, you can imagine the anxiety. The game is thrilling. I see high quality football like never before. I know a thing or two about football – except the offside rule!

Lady Luck is on our side and my team wins. We are riding on cloud nine and singing siNdebele provocative liberation songs. This is what the game of football has become – a political affair. The black and white flags are on show, drivers blow their horns and the town comes to a standstill with jubilation. We arrive back at college and head straight to the dining room, still singing. We are celebrating our win. The game was no pushover. The other team was strong and fought tooth and nail.

I join the queue to get my dinner and another student speaks to me, 'Mr ---- says you should take off your hat while you are in the dining room.' Picture this: the lecturer sending a message is a Shona lecturer, and so is this student. My team has just won a major cup game, and guess what, the hat I'm wearing is my team's hat. *Is this not asking for trouble?* Well as soon as this student stops talking to me I see red. Unfortunately for the student and the lecturer, my friends are listening and trouble sets in. I tell them to butt out as this is my battle and I want to deal with it my way.

'Go and tell Mr ----- he can stick his stinking face where God's sun doesn't shine.' Themba and Dave are on him. They are ready to do damage to him. Before they do, I tell them not to bother as he is not worth them laying their hands on him.

Next it's the lecturer who gets it in the neck. I tell him he is pathetic and not worthy to stand in front of students. He looks at me as if he cannot believe what I am saying. I confirm my statement and tell him I will be reporting him. That makes him uneasy and, believe you me, I mean it. He knows 'spears' will be drawn along tribal lines and he has definitely crossed that sacred line. The boys set upon lecturer, and treat him to a few choice words. *Ground, open up and swallow this man and save him from this embarrassment*! When we are satisfied we have put this lecturer in his place, we sit down and eat our dinner, occasionally breaking into song. Such occurrences become the order of the day during college years.

Another incident in the dining hall on a different day. It all seems to happen or start in the dining hall. A student approaches a group of friends sitting on the other side of the dining table to have their meal. He politely asks for the salt, and I assure you he could not have asked for any more politeness. His mistake, bless him, is that he speaks to this group in Shona. Now that is a big mistake especially where Themba is concerned. How dare he assume this group speaks or understands his language?

Of course they understand him, but you see the political situation is making people so sensitive and intolerant of each other. Themba, being the fiery one, responds, '*Cela ngesiNdebele wena.*' Even by anybody's standards that is low of our Themba. What he calls this guy is a derogatory term and those around him are disappointed. I hand over the salt shaker and attempt to smooth things over. We rebuke Themba and tell him there is no need to be vulgar. College years roll on.

Where Is The Man I Love?

Where has your beloved gone, most beautiful of women?
Which way did your beloved turn, that we may look for
him with you?
Song of Songs 6 vs 1

October 19 1986, breaking news: Samora Machel, president of Mozambique has died in a plane accident. He is one of Robert Mugabe's (Bob, as he has become known) friends. The news is devastating. The continent of Africa reels at the loss of one of their greatest sons.

Conspiracy theories surrounding his death quickly emerge. One of the theories is that his plane has been shot and brought down. To show our solidarity with the Mozambiquan people, it is felt all students should stage coordinated marches. I truly don't know where the idea comes from. There is so much anger and those who decide not to take part are threatened. Instead of rallying together in solidarity with our fellow Africans mourning one of its sons, tribal and party lines take centre stage and others refuse to take part in the march. Most of the Shona-speaking students feel an allegiance towards Machel, while those of us who are siNdebele, while we still feel the pain of death, don't see why we should be part of this. Again this is all politicised based on the goings on in our own country. A rift widens the lines that divides us.

You see, Reader, students or young people have power.

They should never be underestimated. When young people run riot it is nasty. They are a voice to reckon with and they can hardly be silenced. The summer riots of 2010 in the UK are a testament to this and who can forget the Soweto uprising of 16 June 1976?

As college takes centre stage, home visits are few and far between. There is a pressing need to concentrate, produce good results and ensure I pass my first year. I only visit if I want to make a withdrawal from the bank of Mum and Dad; remember that bank, Reader? It never runs out of money, it always gives. Now your kids ask you for money and you roll your eyes and think, *Do they believe money grows on trees?* That is how your mum and dad felt then, and they dared to tell you they did not have any to give you, so deal with it.

Church is part of who I am, and I make no apologies for that. When I'm home I go to my local church. There is a rather quiet, tall, dark, handsome guy amongst the young men in church. He is not easily noticeable. He speaks only when it's necessary. He speaks poshly and is pretty smart too. His use of words I find very attractive. So now you know one of the things I find attractive in a man. Occasionally we talk, pass pleasantries and that's about all. When you get to know him he is a very genuine guy. He is a brilliant story teller.

On different occasions I catch him stealing a glance at me. I ignore him, and think, what on earth are you up to? He finally plucks up courage and spills his feelings. *What took you so long, man?* Time goes by and we start dating. We get closer and closer and enjoy each other's company. I am the envy of many girls. Many girls had eyes on him. *Sorry girls, he has chosen me.*

I am a bit grown up now and know some stuff about this 'love thing'. Love is inborn, and we all have the capacity to grow in love. This time, I will grow in love. Kyle is his name. He is a very special part of my life. We play the love thing pretty smartly.

Preserving my virginity is a big part of me. I want to do this for me and nobody else. Kyle knows that and he never attempts to cross that line. That is the measure I am using to see if he is worth my while. Any hint to pressure me into having sex with him, trust me, gorgeous as he is, that would be it between the two of us. Kyle holds down a highly pressurised job. He has to make big decisions, attend top level board meetings. Amidst his work schedule and my college demands, we do find decent time for each other.

Tables turn. Now that there is a boyfriend on the scene, I'm suddenly home a lot during weekends so we can spend time together. He visits fairly frequently at college too. One normal Sabbath afternoon, we have just finished a youth Bible study and head to his house before he drops me back at college later. He shares the house with his big brother. We socialise with his brother and his wife, and play a game of cards. Somehow his brother and his wife decide they are going out for a little drive. We say our goodbyes and they leave us alone in the house. We mess about, and suddenly we both have the strong urge to get close. In the heat of the moment we both manage to pull away from each other. We are of course disappointed we do not go the whole way, but by the same token glad we manage to restrain ourselves.

'Remember we want to keep the white dress pure,' he says.

Stuff the white dress! I am yelling within myself. Don't be under the illusion restraining myself is a walk in the park, it's torture. Every time we almost come close to giving into our fleshly desires we would both think of 'the white dress'. To every young lady or girl who might be reading this, it is still very possible even in this highly sexualised 21st century to keep yourself and preserve yourself for your wedding night. The desires will come and they will be strong, I mean *strong*. You can overcome. Purpose in your heart, and victory will be yours. I am a young lady in love with a lovely man, a career in education slowly taking shape, what more can a girl wish for? Life is good.

Kyle is a brilliant time keeper just like myself, you see I also find that very attractive about him. People who cannot keep time get on my nerves. We have made plans to go out for dinner during this week when both our schedules allow it. I scrub up well, dress up and wait for my knight in shining armour to come and whisk me off.

He is a no show. There has to be a genuine reason for this as this is so out of character. This guy is always on time. No message, no contact at all. Something is wrong. With my tail between my legs I walk back to my room. I make sure none of my friends find out I have just been stood up. Straight into bed and after much tossing and turning I drift into worlds unknown.

Morning breaks, and it will soon be lectures as usual. Nobody is any the wiser about how I'm feeling. In the first comfort break, I head for the telephone booth and call his workplace. They have not heard from him either and they are worried. I maintain a reasonable level of calm.

Next, his family. I call one of his sisters and she is very shifty with me, and now I am really worried. Something does not quite add up here. My next port of call is his brother, Andrew, and I resolve if I want to get a straight answer I will have to see him one on one.

The only place I can see Andrew for now is my local church. He also has a busy work schedule during the week, so going to his house wouldn't work. Friday of that week can't come soon enough. Friday comes and I head home for the weekend. This time, I'm not after the bank of Mum and Dad, I'm a girl on a mission to find the man she loves.

Saturday morning, I keep things normal and leave for church. Today church is not about my spiritual growth, it's for selfish reasons. I need answers and I need them as of yesterday.

My eyes can see the preacher clearly, but I'm not hearing any words he says. His words sound mumbled. All I want is for him to say the closing prayer, so I can get the chance to speak to Andrew.

'I have not heard from Kyle for three days. What is going on here?'

Andrew looks at me with pitiful eyes, and he scares me. Instead of answering me, he holds my hand and leads me to his car. We sit in the car and I'm nervous.

'Amanda, Kyle is not well,' he says.

I don't know what to say to that. I keep quiet for few seconds.

'Has no one from the family said anything to you?'

'But you are part of the family,' I remind him.

He holds my hand again and squeezes it. He hugs and holds me close. Nobody speaks.

When he finally plucks up the courage, he unleashes a bomb shell. 'Kyle's mental health suddenly deteriorated during the previous week.'

My chest starts to compress. Suddenly, the car appears to not have sufficient air for me to breathe. I am gasping for air, and the life seems to be sucked out of me. Andrew holds my hand and his wife joins us in the car. She says not a word, but embraces me as I cry my eyes out.

'Please can I see him, I want to see him, why did you lot not . . .?' I don't finish my sentence. Again I am gasping for air.

'He is in a pretty bad state.'

'At the moment, Mum, Dad and I are the only ones visiting him.'

'We know how much you love him and how much you would like to see him right now. The family has taken this decision to protect you and him.' Andrew goes on and on.

Whatever else he says, I have no clue. All I want is my Kyle. I want to hold him and look into his eyes. *How is being stopped from seeing my Kyle protecting him?*

Kyle has been a stable, steady guy. There has been no indication of any non-coherence, no indication of an unstable mind, or mental issues. He is the guy that loves life; he laughs, jokes and takes everything in his stride. I almost send myself to an early grave thinking and wondering if I missed any tell-tale signs. For the life of me I can't think of any.

It turns out the pressure at work is the straw that breaks him. He keeps it all in and hopes he will be able to deal with it. Life is a pressure cooker. When it all becomes too much for you, seek help, talk to your trusted friends. Don't be afraid to cry for help. After all, you are human.

When each morning you wake up and you are clothed in your sound mind, be thankful. Many wake up each day and they don't have that luxury, and how they long to see things clearly. *Lord, today I thank you for the sound mind you have given me. Forgive me for thinking it is my right to have my sound mind. I commit all of my brothers and sisters who suffer mental health issues. I seek healing for them. Amen.*

Andrew promises to keep me in the loop on Kyle's progress. The invite to visit my Kyle never comes. I wait patiently. Two weeks go by and no contact. I agonise in silence. I'm sure it's evident to my friends that I am an emotional wreck. I say not a word to any living soul. I fabricate a story: 'Kyle has gone on a work assignment abroad.'

My sadness is put down to the fact that I am missing Kyle. That's fine, the fabrication is serving its purpose. Being at college is torture and I hate everything about it right now. *Maybe if I get to visit him he might get better, what type of woman does he think I am? I'm not there for him at his point of need?*

Another week has passed. I receive a letter from Kyle. Andrew brings it to me at college. Guess what, he is coming from a visit to Kyle. *Yes!* This is Kyle's handwriting. I am happy and scared at the same time. I have also kept a diary for myself since he's been away. I will share it with him. After all it's about my feelings since he's been away. I can't wait to read my letter.

Andrew says his goodbyes, and tells me he has been ordered to take me out to dinner. Even from his sick bed, Kyle is thinking of me. Tomorrow I am going for dinner with Andrew. The idea is not exciting at all. I should be going out with my Kyle and not his brother. Nonetheless, I accept the invite and I know Kyle would be happy to learn I have respected his wish.

I love you, and remember the white dress. That is the full content of the letter from Kyle. Truthfully I don't know how to react. By now tears are dropping in bucketloads. Well, I pull myself together and attempt a bit of revision and tell myself that tomorrow will be a better day.

After eight weeks Kyle is out of hospital. I don't know how I'm expected to react to the news since I have not visited once and it is not for the lack of trying. Two days after his discharge he comes to visit me at college. There isn't much change in his demeanour and appearance apart from the fact that he has lost a significant amount of weight. The initial reaction from both of us is to embrace, kiss and cry for a good few minutes without exchanging any words. *To hell with the afternoon lectures, I am spending the afternoon with my Kyle.* I am deliberate in not asking him how he is feeling, at least for now. We talk about general stuff and leave it there.

'Can we go out for dinner tomorrow after you finish lectures?' he asks.

'I guess we can,' I respond.

'I promise not to stand you up this time.'

Well, the man still has his sense of humour. Which is amazing, considering recent events.

'If you stand me up this time . . .' Before I complete my sentence he gives me one big smacker of a kiss and it shuts me up.

Tomorrow comes, and he is dead on time. He picks me up and off we go. He has reserved a table for two in this lovely restaurant. Again it's general chit chat as we enjoy the meal. A few minutes into our dessert, he asks me that dreaded question. It is direct and requires a direct answer.

'Why did you not visit me while in hospital?'

I look up and stare at him. Surely this man must know that was something out of my control? I instantly lose my appetite for my dessert. I play around with my spoon and he fires the question again. This time I answer him.

'I was not allowed to visit.'

'What do you mean you were not allowed?'

I go through the pain of explaining what was said to me and all that went on, and how I tried to convince his brother how important it was for me to visit. Trying to explain myself reawakens all the raw emotions I have been going through for the last two months, and really I had not expected to be taken there yet.

'But I needed you. I wanted to see you. I wanted you to tell me things would be all right.'

Now this is torture.

'I wanted to see you too, Kyle. I wanted to be there next to you every day you spent in hospital. I was told that was a family . . .' By now I am sobbing. This feels so wrong. I pull myself together after a few sobs. 'I had to respect your family's wishes.'

'How come Andrew never told me this?' he asks.

'Well you should take it up with him and not me.'

'I needed you next to me, Amanda,' he says once again.

'And I wanted to be next to you,' I respond. A prolonged silence.

We put that to bed and vow to go on. As time goes on it becomes apparent we have both been damaged by this whole thing and it has ruptured our relationship. We both try to get over it and rebuild but it is just not happening. He argues I should not have listened to his family. I feel I was not in a position to disregard his family's wishes. I carry the guilt while he seems to have unanswered questions. We struggle to reconnect and moving on is a challenge. We can both kid ourselves and hope all will be OK, and if we give it time, we will get back to how things were.

After months we both do what's honourable and end the relationship. Oh, Reader, it is painful. Painful because we both still love each other, but under the circumstances it's the best thing to do. They say time heals, and hopefully we will heal from this. Such is life, folks. It takes you to places you never want to be.

Now a parent myself, I do empathise with Kyle's parents. I understand their decision. Their decision was taken out of love and not malice. They felt the need to protect him, especially from the stigma attached to mental health issues, and I believe they also had my best interests at heart. The decision was not meant to break us up. Kyle and I had the choice to make things work but we did not know how.

Kyle later meets somebody, and they have a daughter. Guess what, Reader: his daughter is called Amanda. I am shocked and flattered at the same time.

'What did you do that for?' I ask him when we coincidentally bump into each other years after.

'Let's just say I never stopped loving you.'

'Does your wife know the history behind that name?'

He tells me his wife knew about it two years after having the child, and that she was not pleased. What woman would be? The men I have dated have a thing about my second name. Well, Kyle, that's no skin off my nose, you can deal with any comeuppance. I wonder how he would react if they had a son and his wife named him after one of her exes. Kyle goes into my book of memories.

'Never give up on someone with a mental illness. When 'I' is replaced by 'We', illness becomes wellness.'
Shannon L. Alder

A Blast From The Past

'Sometimes when people leave it usually is for the better.
Just because they left doesn't mean that they are gone
forever. One day when you're least expecting it they come
back into your life. As a miracle or a blessing!'
Junie Morgan

'Hi, Amanda.' I turn round and there he is. Alfred. A good four or so years have passed since I last had any contact. I'm walking home with my friends after church, having been home for the weekend.

I exchange pleasantries with this 'stalker', only he is not that type of stalker. There is little said between the two of us. He is now an accountant and works for a mining company. After the weekend I head back to college.

Thank God it's Friday again. A little respite from lectures is most welcome. Chantelle invites me to her church worship programme taking place at the college chapel. As soon as we get inside I feel very uncomfortable. The way of worship is different to what I'm used to. There is so much screaming and shouting. It's a frenzy.

Chantelle joins in this mayhem and she appears very comfortable with it. I hardly recognise the songs being sung. Some people are crying and screaming at the top of their voices and speaking in a strange way. Others are banging their heads on the walls, the pastor appears to be rebuking people, and I just can't work out what type of worship this is.

As though rehearsed, everybody suddenly forms a circle, and the pastor and three men stand in the middle. I'm more confused. The pastor and the three men in the middle place their hands on people's foreheads and appear to be pushing them backwards and people start falling to the floor. It's like coconuts falling off a tree.

My turn comes, hands are laid on my forehand. I'm pushed and surprisingly I don't fall. I'm pushed harder and nothing happens. The pastor looks me in the eye, I look back at him hard as he does, and he leaves me and moves on to the next person.

By now I have had enough of this, so I quietly sneak out and leave. The level of noise gives me a headache so severe I miss lectures for two days. Chantelle and I never discuss this.

Another day in college, lectures as usual, no big deal.

'Regina you have a phone call in Albert Hall,' another student calls out to me. 'I told the person to call you at 3.20 as we would be having a break from our psychology lecture.'

The fifteen-minute break from a boring lesson finally comes. Psychology is not a dull subject, but the lecturer for that day is dead boring! I head straight for the telephone booth and wait for the call. On the dot the phone rings.

'Hello, Regina speaking.'

'Hi, Amanda,' says the voice.

'Oh hi, Kyle,' I blurt out.

'I'm not Kyle,' says the voice. Silence. Now I'm confused as to who the voice is.

'Who is this?' I ask.

'It's Alfred,' the voice identifies itself.

'Oh, Alfred, how are you? You sounded like my friend Kyle.'

'Only I am not your friend Kyle.'

That remark makes me feel awkward, and I want the ground to swallow me. 'Whatever, Alfred! How are you?' We both laugh.

'Would you like to go out for dinner this Saturday evening?'

'This Saturday is not a good day for me.' I have exams coming up the following week so my Saturday evening is already booked. We settle for a Saturday in a fortnight. The next week and a half is spent with my head down, studying hard, and preparing for impending exams.

That Saturday finally comes. Exams are over and hurray, I have passed. The first dinner date is followed by another, then another, and many more after that. Now I'm asking myself what exactly I had with this man the first time when I was still a high-school pupil. It was nothing other than infatuation. Now I'm confident that I know a thing or two about love. Once again, I get a chance to fall in love.

Teaching Practice

A teacher who loves learning earns the right and the ability to help others learn.'
Ruth Beechick,

My first teaching experience is intimidating. The first day is particularly daunting. The only solace is I'm not yet totally responsible for a full class. My mentor is there and is in charge. She senses my intimidation and offers words of encouragement.

'It's normal to feel intimidated for the first time in front of children,' she tells me.

The first three-week placement is over, and I'm glad. Very soon I will be faced with a full year placement and I will be in charge of a class of between thirty five to forty five children. Somebody give me strength.

All students dread the full-year teaching placement. We are placed in remote areas of the country. Nobody wants to teach in those areas, but unfortunately somebody has to. Children in those areas have the right to education too. Being posted to those areas means less visits to your family and loved ones. Depending on the weather, public transport might come to a halt because of flooding rivers. The preserve of acquiring a town placement is for those that are married and have families; the axe will fall on the likes of me.

Corruption within the civil service is rife. 'Bottom power'

plays a massive part in determining where you are placed. Female students having affairs with lecturers know they are well set. Sexual favours guarantee placement in the city. Now, Reader, this is referred to as 'bottom power'. Strong medical reasons are also considered. I'm not sleeping with any lecturer, I'm not married, and neither do I have a medical condition, so you can understand my concern. I am scared to my wits' end. I'm not cut out to be teaching in some remote village at the back of beyond. There are many worrying stories about these areas; for example, if one of the villagers is interested in a female student teacher and the student teacher is not interested, it is said the villager will use some sort of witchcraft on them. Without realising it, the student finds themselves in a relationship. I find that very disturbing.

My placement letter finally lands through the door. I open it. Mama is standing by and is also anxious. I scan the letter and all I can see is the name of the school, Chikandabubi. That name alone is enough to depress me. Confirming my suspicions, it's at the back of beyond and I hear scary stories about the area. Some say the villagers practise witchcraft and transport is in short supply.

My eldest brother's girlfriend works for the Ministry of Education. She is not in a position to influence any decisions but I approach her and beg her to see if she can do something for me. She makes no promises.

Two weeks prior to schools commencing in the new year she calls me and informs me she has managed to help secure a new placement. Before I start celebrating, I wait until I receive the new confirmation letter. I have now been posted to Masuku Primary school. There will be three other students from the same college; at least I will have peers to compare notes.

The placement commences in January 1987. I don't

receive any payment for three months. I know it will be backdated so I am not worried. Three months' pay will be some windfall, Reader. I am thinking trips to the hairdresser, handbags, shoes and more shoes. The windfall finally lands, I am the richest girl living, at least in my opinion.

Now we have a tradition in my family, and the prospect of countless pairs of shoes is not strong enough for me to break this family tradition. My two brothers did it and I want to carry it on. I don't know its roots, but it is highly esteemed within the family. Each child shares their first pay cheque with the rest of the family. In later years, Mama explains that she is teaching us to value family more than money. Brilliant lesson, Mama! I will be passing this family tradition to my children.

Placement year is spent marking children's books, lesson plans, spending time with family and of course the man I love. I learn a lot about children, family structures and what makes a good teacher. Before I realise it, the year is over and the following year it's back to college.

You Have Crossed The Line, Mr Lecturer

'I hope each and every one of you reach for the stars and land among the clouds. You have one life, one body. Take care of it, own it. Live it and love it. Live your life to the fullest without being reckless.'
Bonnie Zackson Koury

1988, I'm back at college for my third year. The year rolls by, and tensions between students from the two tribes is still evident. Lecturers also get involved. The divide is clear. Some students claim they are deliberately being failed on the basis of their tribe. I never experience that. Corruption is on the rise, especially in high places. Love affairs between students and lecturers are also rampant. Most of them are not a question of love. Girls sell themselves short so they pass their course. Lecturers do it because they feel they have absolute power over their students.

There is a very disturbing open secret making the rounds; apparently one of the clerical staff (librarian) is helping female students with illegal and dangerous abortions. Some say he is some sort of herbalist, and others claim that for him to initiate the process, female students have to have sex with him first. How low can humanity fall?

Students spend a considerable amount of time at the library, some more than others. I'm one of those who frequent the library maybe more than necessary. Doing that you see, Reader, a girlfriend wanting a chat cannot disturb me.

It would appear, at least in the herbalist's twisted mind, that I have put on weight. I don't notice any changes in my weight. This herbalist guy can be a bit too friendly at times. Others like it, I don't. I know how to deal with him, and I ignore the idiot. Each time I am in the library he volunteers to help me find reference books that are a bit tricky to find. His niceness goes on for about a fortnight. I cut down on my library visits as he is now making me uncomfortable.

I have a library book that is due back but I still need to use it, so I have no choice but to go to the library and get an extension. He is behind the desk. The library is less busy and he is practically alone. He is his usual, friendly self. He strikes up a conversation. Nothing wrong with that.

'You don't have to drop out of college at this time?'

I am confused by his statement. 'Excuse me, what are you talking about?'

'You know what I mean, I can help you sort things out.'

I look at this man, not sure I'm following him. Then the penny drops. He suspects that I am pregnant and he has basically just offered me an abortion. I feel sick and want to slap him big time.

Honestly speaking you don't want to know the words that came out of my mouth to that horrible specimen of a man. I feel violated. He brags that nobody will believe me even if I tell. I share this with one good friend who advises me not to take it further as I will not be believed. Reluctantly, I follow that advice.

Another third-year student is rumoured to be pregnant and has apparently shared her circumstance with a friend. She confides she is having an abortion. It's a shame the trusted friend is not a truly trustworthy friend because she shares the secret.

It's a Sunday and most students are off campus for the weekend. The rumoured pregnant student is at college as well. I live in the same halls of residence as her. As I come out of my room en-route to the television room, I spot the librarian sneaking into her room. I proceed with my plans for the day and try not to think about what might have been happening in this girl's room.

By the end of the day an ambulance is called for her. She is bleeding heavily and her life hangs in the balance. Rumours start making the rounds. I don't say a word about what I saw earlier; after all it's none of my business, but nonetheless I feel angry and upset about the whole thing. Unfortunately, we continue with our lives regardless

It's a Friday evening at college and I am in my room minding my own business. It's hot and very uncomfortable. A girlfriend comes over for a chat. We chat and laugh, order pizza and chat more. She leaves my room well after 10 p.m. I tidy up my room and get myself ready for bed. I have not yet locked my door.

Suddenly the door handle moves, but I'm not startled by it as I think that my girlfriend has decided to come back for more chit chat. Surprise surprise, one of the lecturers launches himself into my room.

I jump up and stand in the middle of the room. The man is drunk, and has no business being in my room. I ask him to leave and he ignores me. By now I'm hysterical, and I'm yelling at him. He mumbles something. I loathe the man, and if he is the last man standing, sorry Reader, right now, the human race will have to come to an end.

I let out one big scream that frightens him and he scarpers out of my room so fast. I also leave my room crying and in shock. I go to a friend's room and explain what just happened. I crush in with my friend for the night.

News is spread of a certain lecturer seen leaving a student's room and there are multiple versions of what really happened. Others say the student has been two-timing the lecturer. I am dying to set the record straight but decide against it. I don't want to jeopardise anything as I make up my mind I will be reporting this to the college dean. My weekend is ruined, and I cancel a date with Alfred and come up with a lame excuse. I'm tempted to tell him what has taken place, but a still, small voice cautions me. This is my battle, and I will deal with it.

'Why are you worried? You know the truth,' my friend Melissa consoles me.

'It's well and good for you to say this, people will not believe me!' I burst out crying.

Monday can't come soon enough so I can tell my story to the principal himself. Now, there is a huge problem here. Because of the tribal divide, every mishap is analysed and judged as such, whether deserving or not. The lecturer is Shona, and I am Ndebele. *So what business has he got with a Ndebele student?* This and questions like it will be asked, and trust me they will be. Did he think he would treat me as his dirty stop out and disrespect me? Let's find out. You have picked on the wrong one, Mr Lecturer. You have stirred up a hornet's nest! Spears will dissect your body when this goes out, come Monday.

Monday comes and I head straight to one of my favourite lecturers and I relay the events.

'Are you sure there is nothing untoward going on between you and Mr M?' You see he wants to be sure of the facts before he deals with the matter.

I assure him there is nothing going on and I also tell him I am in a relationship with someone. After he has satisfied himself through thorough questioning, he takes the matter on.

What I have just recounted to the lecturer is like handing a hungry lion a piece of meat. Ndebele lecturers are summoned. Most of them turn up and I am forced to recount the events again. This is now becoming torture. They all want to make sure I'm not hiding anything.

Two days later, I am called into the principal's office and a few lecturers are present including Mr M. It is concluded that Mr M's behaviour was unacceptable and that personal and professional lines have been crossed. The recommendation is for him to be suspended pending further investigations.

Boring Tradition, Unrealistic Parents!

'We never know the love of a parent till we become
parents ourselves.'
Henry Ward Beecher

In a few days I will the big Two-One. I don't want any fuss
really. Let it come and go. I'm sure there will be no key. *In
their eyes what is it that I need to open or unlock? I'm
sure they want everything to remain locked.* Strangely
enough I do receive the traditional twenty-first key, only
it's not from my parents. I receive it from Alfred.

Now I have a dilemma in my hands. Where do I keep
this key and who do I say bought the key? My parents are
hardcore Africans. One does not just turn up with such
stuff and expect them to be cool. Not in an African home,
at least not when I was growing up.

So what does a girl do in such instances? I approach my
second eldest brother, and explain my dilemma. We
concoct a story. My brother is now the purchaser of the
key. Deal done. My secret is safe. Every girl needs a
brother. The key is accompanied by a message. *Amanda,
unlock the door to your heart and let me in.*

The relationship grows and blossoms and after a couple
years of dating, I officially introduce him to my parents.

*

Our parents are in our lives so they can accomplish their God-given responsibility to mentor, nurture and protect us, and as such they deserve all our respect. My parents have never been different.

Culture is who we are as a people, without it we don't know who we really are.

Once Alfred is officially introduced to my parents and his intentions to marry me made known, a process has to begin. Marriage in my culture has to bring the two families together, and solid relationships are made.

There is what is called lobola, some call it the bride price or dowry, which is paid by the bridegroom's family to the bride's.

The two families meet up and the process is initiated. My parents are very reasonable as to what they expect from Alfred's family for the lobola. They don't make this a business transaction or abuse it as others have. I am proud they love me so much and are happy I have found the man of my dreams.

During my courtship with Alfred, little red flags spring up and cause me a bit of concern. I am quick to dismiss them. Mama is aware of my concerns, and she asks me questions. Her line of questioning, at the time, is annoying me. She wants me to be truthful to myself and to her. This goes on for what seems like eternity. I go on the defensive, and I am not going to let her in on my concerns, lest she persuade me to leave my man. I know she is talking to my dad over the issue. Mum and dad just want a few things clarified before I commit myself.

Right now, as far as I am concerned, Alfred is the man for me and nobody is going to stop me from being with him. Dad speaks to me as well. They are not saying I shouldn't be with him, after all they have accepted him and given their approval for my hand in marriage.

I fall out with Mama over their 'unrealistic and unfounded concerns'. Within a week of the big fall out with my mama, I move in with Alfred.

This move goes against everything I stand for and believe in. Every thread within my body knows I shouldn't be doing this, it's just not what I'm cut out to do. It defies all reason that I have done this, but right now I don't care. My heart is ruling my head, and trust me it feels so good to do what I think is right for me.

Trying to rid myself of the guilt, I rationalise my behaviour and sure enough my reasons seem justifiable. All of a sudden, my parents are not cool enough, not educated enough to my liking, I think they have not moved on with the world, so I'm moving on and leaving them behind. That is what I tell myself in an attempt to make sense of my insane, careless and somewhat dangerous decision.

Mama says not a word as I pack my belongings and say my goodbyes.

Alfred knows this living arrangement is ripping me apart. I am not at peace with myself, my conscience is tormenting me. The guilt I carry is beyond words.

We both want to be legally married, so we make plans. It is not the big fairy tale wedding that I had dreamt of as a young girl.

None of us can ever outsmart our parents, we can never be wiser than them, and no matter how our lives pan out, I will always need my parents and I am ever so thankful for their forgiveness towards me. I never at any stage heard the words, 'we told you so'.

For Better Or Worse.
New School; New Challenges

*For this reason a man will leave his father and mother
and be united to his wife, and the two will become one
flesh. So they are no longer two, but one flesh. Therefore,
what God has joined together, let no one separate.'*
Matthew 19 vs 5-6 '

First of March 1991. On that day I vow, 'For better or
worse, for richer for poor till death do us part.'

I am now a qualified teacher, teaching at a remote school
in one of the areas that was a trouble spot during the civil
unrests in Zimbabwe. It's a normal school day and I teach
the sixth grade. Suddenly one of my pupils jumps out of
his chair as one possessed. He screams and runs around
the classroom shouting, 'No, no, Mama!'

He runs towards me and wraps his arms around me. I
hold him tight, and I ask the rest of the class to leave the
classroom and to raise the alarm. The poor boy is now
foaming at the mouth and he is trying to tell me something
but I cannot understand a word he says. I whisper a prayer
or something close to a prayer. He tightens his grip around
my waist so that it hurts. The experience is frightening.

One of the teachers comes to the rescue. He grabs the
boy and puts him on the floor and tells me not to touch
him. I struggle with that. The boy needs human touch and

some form of assurance, how can I deny him that priceless gift: unconditional human contact?

Later on, I am told the poor boy witnessed his pregnant mother's tummy being slashed open by the Gugurahundi during the unrests in the country. I call him boy, but he is almost a grown man. War prevented him attending school at the usual time. He is suffering flashbacks of the incident. I hope he finally found peace and the help he needed to cope with that trauma. This is my first encounter with Post-Traumatic Stress Disorder.

The second school term of 1991 is due to commence in mid-April. I have been married for a month and no surprises, already a few weeks pregnant. There was no wasting time on that front! We are both excited and happy. Only one thing stands in the way of our happiness: I am teaching in a rural school, and that means being away from each other for most of the time.

Two weeks before I'm due to go back to school, we both decide to do something about this issue. We make an appointment to see the education officer in charge of placements.

'Yes, young lady, how can I help today?' the officer asks me.

'I need you to consider me for a town placement,' I respond.

'Have your circumstances changed recently?' he asks. He is looking at me above his glasses. Alfred is sitting next to me and I can see that he is starting to get fidgety. I explain to him that I recently married and I'm pregnant. He plays around with his pens and shuffles his papers. It's rather annoying.

The man is rather rude in his response. He informs us there is nothing unique with my change of circumstance.

Well, that's it. Alfred has been riled up and he quickly responds to him. There is no beating about the bush. Realising he is not paying attention to us, we call his bluff and request a resignation form. Now he does pay attention. He was not expecting that sort of request.

'But, Mr Ncube, we need qualified teachers in the field.' He chooses to address Alfred and not me. *Hello, I'm the teacher here not him*!

After intense negotiations he finally succumbs. Our little psychology tricks pay dividends. Would you believe it; he places me back in the same school where I did my second-year placement. What are the odds of that happening?

The new term starts and I'm heading back to my not-so-new school. I'm glad there will be no intense introductions and many a familiar face. Interestingly, the headmaster pretends he can't remember me. I find that a bit bizarre. You see, the man had made a pass at me when I was a student teacher. The silly old fool must have done this so many times he wouldn't remember whom he approached. Oh, maybe his ego is bruised since I turned him down. This is going to be a challenging working relationship. Girlfriends, please don't sell yourselves short to any undeserving men.

Such behaviour is common from those in positions of authority. They behave like an old boys' club. *Let him dare approach me again this time, he will regret the day he was born*. As I suspect, he approaches me and I give him my piece of mind, a few home truths and, oh boy, have I just started a war.

Settling into my new role is no issue at all. I get on with the job in hand and all is good until a new pay rise system is introduced. The new system gives headmasters the power to assess you and determine if you qualify for a raise or not. It goes without saying, this will be subject to abuse. I know straightaway I will have to fight tooth and nail to get assessed, and later on to be approved for the pay rise.

Within a year virtually every teacher in my school is assessed and gets a raise except for a few others and myself.

Almost two years into the new system, he still does not appraise me. Somehow I'm not that worried about it. I have this belief that what is rightfully mine will come my way at the right time.

One normal payday I get my payslip and when I look, I see figures that appear inflated. Guess what, my pay has been amended not by the headmaster, but by a higher power that none of us can oppose. Experience teaches me that if deserving of something, you don't always have to put up a fight. Sometimes it's best to let go and continue with life. What is meant for you will finally land in your path. No circumstance or strong blowing wind can take you away from its reach. I am not talking about deliberately missing opportunities, though. When opportunities present themselves, go all out and grab them.

Married Life: Mother-in-Law's First Visit

Throughout life people will make you mad, disrespect you and treat you bad. Let God deal with the things they do, 'cause hate in your heart will consume you too.
Will Smith

Married life is good. We are no different to any other couple, so we make plans to better ourselves and our home. Part of these plans obviously include finances. We get a joint account for our savings and other emergencies. Is there anything wrong with that? In recent years there has been many a debate on whether this is the way forward in a fast changing society. My honest answer is there is nothing wrong with that if it works for you. I still don't have the right answer as to whether a married couple should have one account or not but what I can say is that if it works for you why not? After all, the vows say for better or for worse.

A significant time into that arrangement I suddenly realise that a few things don't add up. I find that I am having to justify myself more where finances are concerned. Something is definitely wrong, let me wait and see. I am around six months pregnant at the time and my hormones are all over the place. Talk of being a tearful wreck. Anything is enough to set me off, from a tear-jerker movie to witnessing a toddler throw a tantrum in the middle of a department store.

Not wanting to discuss this I quietly take the financial matter into my own hands. I do what I think I need to do without making any song and dance over it. Maybe I'm wrong here but I have to do something. Am I asking for a proper first row here? Well, I'll see.

He comes home, I know he is gunning for a row. I ignore him and get on with my marking.

A few months down the line my mother-in-law will be visiting. We are both excited at the prospect. I think, *I will do everything in my power, I will go out of my way to make sure she is comfortable and enjoys her stay with us. I am going to be the perfect daughter-in-law.*

She will be with us for a month. It is unfortunate though, that her visit is during the school term, as it means she is home alone for most of the time as we both have to go to work. She is cool with it. I make the most of the time I have with her.

Alfred is her sole provider and this is a responsibility he takes seriously. I admire him for that and I'm proud of him. Someone once said, you can tell if a man is a good one by the way he treats his mother. Is it really true though? All is well and we have a jolly good time with her. She seems happy and I am convinced that if there was a test between mother-in-law and daughter-in-law, I have passed it with flying colours.

A couple of days before my mother-in-law is due to go back to the village, I'm told she has requested some provisions to take back with her. *So what, the old girl has asked for a few provisions, Regina, what's the big deal?*

There is a lot riding on this, Reader. Now let me explain myself before you judge me and certify me as insane. Firstly, custom dictates my mother-in-law must come directly to me with her request and secondly, I did not need reminding at all. She is our responsibility and I know what has to happen. Directing her request to her son is in fact saying she does not recognise her son is now a married man.

What makes it even worse, Alfred should know better and should have directed his mother to me with her request. I make my feelings known to him, throw a big strop, and let him deal with her request. You can put it down to hormones or whatever, I am not being treated fairly here.

He goes on and purchases the groceries, and the mother-in-law heads back to the village. The very night she leaves I am at the receiving end of his reaction.

I have no visible bruises so I go to work in the morning as though nothing has happened. Women, hey! We master the art of putting on different masks to be all things to all people. We brush up and face the world as though nothing is wrong. That takes courage. But the real damage is that which is not visibly seen.

Normally I get home first from work. Surprisingly, today he is home before me. I put my bags away and head for the bathroom for a much needed soak and I indulge myself in bubbles. I struggle to be in the same room as him. After my bath I grab my Danielle Steel novel and immerse myself. Who am I kidding? I can't focus and keep reading the same sentence over and over. I am trying to make sense of last night's events. I have flashbacks.

He comes outside and makes small talk. All I manage is one-word answers. He wants us to go out. I refuse. He pleads and pleads and I refuse. He attempts an apology. Right now I only want my own company. The baby kicks and I try and enjoy that moment between mother and unborn child. Now follows the pathetic, 'Oh I'm sorry, I really don't know what came over me.' I finally accept the apology. Yes, you have read correctly. I forgive him.

I can hear you screaming and sighing and calling me stupid, foolish or idiot. And I hear you saying if that was me I would have packed my bags and left and saying if it was me, I would have done such and such, I would have said this and that. All I can say to you is, '*Really?*'

Until a situation confronts, you just don't know how you would react, especially where matters of the heart are concerned. We like to kid ourselves and believe we would do ABC but the opposite is usually true. So please don't judge me or call me weak; I am simply human and I love this man.

A message to all mothers with sons. I have a son too, and we do have heart-to-heart moments. I talk to him as a woman and as his mother. Help your sons be the best men the world can ever produce. I challenge all mothers to positively empower their boys. I am empowering mine, what about you?

A mother who teaches values to her son, makes him the man she would like her daughter to be married to. A mother who empowers her son, secures his happy future.
Author Unknown

Birth Of A Son

Children are a heritage from the LORD, OFFSPRING *a reward from him. Like arrows in the hands of a warrior are children born in one's youth. Blessed is the man whose quiver is full of them. They will not be put to shame when they contend with their opponents in court.*
Psalms 127 vs3-5

So there's this boy. He kinda stole my heart. He calls me 'Mom'.
Author Unknown

I struggle being around my own family during the first year of my marriage. I am almost becoming a stranger to them. None of them has changed but a lot is happening around me. I am the one who is changing. I know for a fact my mama is worried about me, and I visit her as and when I can.

My pregnancy is progressing without any concerns and soon I will be cradling my baby in my arms. I am huge, my nose is covering my face and my backside resembles the behind of a double decker bus. You know what, all that doesn't matter, soon it will be all over.

For some strange reason, I begin to question who God is in my life and what relationship I have with him. I go to church religiously, I have a good understanding of the

Bible and I am baptised, so what on earth am I having these questions and thoughts for? With what I know about God and being a baptised member of a church that knows the Bible, well, I should be set. It is crystal clear that yes I know of God only as a head knowledge, but I just don't have a relationship with him. So what have I been doing for the twenty four years of my life? To be fair, subtract the growing up years and just look at half of those years. I have been playing church, saving face, playing the religious game, attending church every Sabbath because I didn't know anything else to fill my time on a Sabbath. All this is bugging me right now. I simply dismiss it.

It is December of 1991 and in preparation for the birth of my child I go back to my parents' home before Christmas. Tradition dictates that for the birth of my first child, I go back to my parents. There is nothing sinister about this. The main reason is, I'm not experienced in motherhood, and my mama will be on hand to help and offer real advice and ensure I get the rest I need after childbirth.

It's Saturday the 11th of January 1992. I get up in the morning and I feel a bit of discomfort. My back is painful. I suspect it must be the start of things to come. Mama has gone to church and I am home with my dad and my aunt. Mama comes back home for lunch. She takes one look at me, smiles and says, 'Today is the day.' She is annoying me and my discomfort is making me irritable. Anyone around me seems to be annoying me today. I go through much of the labour at home and around about 8 p.m. it's time to pay the smiling midwives a visit.

By midday of the following day I still have not given birth. I have laboured all night to no avail. Now I'm exhausted and the baby is in distress. A life and death decision has to be made. C-section it has to be. I don't have the option of a natural birth anymore. Two lives hang in the balance.

My blood pressure rockets, and I can hear the doctor talking about the baby's heart rate dropping. Mother Nature is not being fair right now. How I had looked forward to a natural birth. I pinch myself out of that sorry state. I have to be thankful for medical advances making it possible for women to have children should Mother Nature change her course. I get prepared for theatre.

Ready to be wheeled into theatre, my dressing gown falls off to the floor. I ask one of the midwives in attendance if she could pick it up for me. She turns round, looks me in the eye and responds with the equivalent of, 'You must be kidding'. So much for a caring midwife.

One should endeavour to show kindness to people at all times. You never know when you might need help from the very person to whom you have been unkind. People's paths always seem to cross at some point. Years down the line, little do I know the same midwife will need my help. Unbelievable!

I happen to be teaching her little boy one year. A directive is passed to relocate all the children who come from a certain area to a new school and her child is in my class and needs to be relocated. This parent approaches the school to speak to her child's teacher to plead her case against the intended relocation. As I am talking to her I am battling to place her. Her face looks familiar, but where from? She mentions she is a midwife at the same hospital I gave birth to my son. The penny drops!

Her words come buzzing into my ears. I cannot mistake that voice. The voice of a lady who refused to pick up my gown off the floor when I was in labour, and my life and that of my unborn baby hung in the balance. The lady who neglected the very core of her calling. You don't mistake that voice and you remember the face. *Yep! Wait for your comeuppance, lady. Today I am in charge and let's see who rules the roost. Oh how the tables have turned.*

The urge to put her in her rightful place is attractive, logical and overwhelmingly hard to resist. Just before I open my mouth to vomit words of power on her, one of my mama's wise sayings come ringing back to me. 'Remember each person is God's creature, treat them like so.' *Really, Mama will never know*; I try to reason with my selfish motives. The words ring even louder in my head. *At least let me remind her.* I remind her of her behaviour to one pregnant woman on the 12th of January of 1992. The look of embarrassment. She is ashamed and has no words to justify her behaviour. Such is life.

Everyday, learn something however small. Life is for learning. I try to do my best with people. Sometimes I mess up and sometimes I get it right. When we feel like revenge or are confused or are about to do something wrong, there is always that small voice that has a habit of appearing when we don't want it to because if the truth be told, we would rather have it our way. Don't ignore it, it's the voice of reason.

The voice is fuzzy and I can't figure out where I am.

'You have a baby boy.'

Then I remember, I am in the maternity wing and the last I remember the anaesthetist put me to sleep while asking me to count to five. Oh dear, I am a mother now. I behold my son for the first time and there is a gush of love for him from my heart. This little person depends on me. I vow to protect him, to love him and to be the best mother ever. Birth is indeed a miracle.

He lies there, unaware I am enjoying him. I am in hospital for a week. Mama has geared herself for sleepless nights. She has made allowances for baby and mother. She will take care of both. Between her and my sister, they bathe the baby, cook for me, and do all the baby laundry. She guides me through breastfeeding and gets up in the night, checks on us and even picks the baby up if I'm out for the count. Kennedy Mayibongwe is my handsome bundle of joy.

After three months I move back to my own house with our new son. Good old Mama made sure I was strong enough before I went back to my home. All is well.

Control, Control & More Control

You are responsible for how you feel no matter what someone does to you. Remember, you are in control of your thoughts so choose to feel confident and adequate rather than angry and insecure.
Robert Tew

People that abuse are manipulative and controlling, and trust me, they do not come with any labels. If they came with labels no significant other would touch them with a barge pole. They have a way of making you believe what is going on is your fault, and sadly enough you start believing.

The baby occupies my time. Becoming a mother brings about a turning point in my spiritual journey. I come to the realisation all along I have been simply 'playing church' and going through the motions of it all. This time I need a relationship with my maker. Church has a new meaning. It is no longer about the activities that go on. It becomes a place of refuge, a place where I meet with other sinners like me and still leave hopeful. It becomes a place where I can tell God all my joys and fears. God becomes real in my life. I realise one cannot 'do' life on their own. There has to be more to life than what we see, So I have a one to one with God, ask for forgiveness for putting him on the back burner for all these years and ask for his guidance. Well let's wait and see if he will do as I ask.

Alfred appears distant from me. Intimacy is almost dead. On the occasions it happens it is more out of duty than anything else. I'm noticing that even communication is becoming limited. When he talks he is cold, he is putting me down and I don't understand why. Every day I find myself having to take stock of what I have said, how I might have acted, and for the life of me there is nothing that stands out to justify this behaviour. I feel lonely, and I'm scared to talk. My baby boy is the only person keeping me going and facing each day. He smiles and giggles, and I smile back.

Soon I realise my support network has somehow been controlled without me realising. When I talk it ends up in a row and everything is my fault, so I am told. There is so much emotional blackmail, I don't know how to deal with it. I put up with it and hope for the best. Have you ever felt lonely in a world abuzz with people of every kindred and tongue?

Remember, I am also re-establishing my relationship with God, so in my human limited mind I feel I cannot bombard Him with all this. I think I can handle it and I casually talk to Him about it, but not wholeheartedly. I'm sure He knows where I am coming from, I tell myself.

A new teacher joins the school. There is an instant attraction between the two of us. We connect, and we get each other. I am thinking, where have you been all my life? I could definitely use someone like you. The individual is a good listener. We become very close, in fact dangerously close. That is what I need. I can almost sense your disappointment in me, Reader. Sorry to disappoint you, it's not another man it's a good girlfriend. God rest her soul.

She invites me out for lunch one weekend to one of her friends' houses. A good natter with other girls might do me good. More women arrive. At my last count, there are fifteen of us in the room. We talk, we put the world to rights, we talk shoes, hairdressers and handbags.

These women are a free spirited bunch. Some of them have no qualms sharing intimate and personal stuff. There is such a sisterhood, a spirit of oneness I've never seen before. Well, I am justified in not sharing anything; after all I don't know them that well. It is so refreshing, though, to see women share so freely without any fear of being judged. Girls have the power to empower each other, let's please learn to be there for each other. Who better to understand another woman's problems than a woman?

In the process, it is decided a burial society to help in times of bereavement should be formed. Within a month of that day the society is up and running. To date the society continues to grow from strength to strength.

Next time you make contact with another sister and they say they are fine, go home and say a prayer for them, for the opposite is true. They are not fine; they want someone to reach out to them. You can never tell how far your prayer goes. I believe I have kept sane by the prayers that have been said on my behalf without my knowledge.

Second Chances

'The weak can never forgive. Forgiveness is the attribute
of the strong.'
Mahatma Gandhi

'Amanda, I think we need to talk.'

A heart to heart takes place between Alfred and me. It is a no-holds-barred type of discussion. Each is open and honest. It's uncomfortable but it needs to happen. It goes on and on till the wee hours of the morning. There are tears, hugs and kisses and all is forgiven.

Everybody deserves a second chance. Judge whichever way you wish. Love isn't like a tap for us to turn on and off. Love lingers on even beyond terrible pain. I love the man so I forgive him. I want to do all in my power to save my marriage. Things change massively and we are back on track and we are happy. There is more communication, romantic gestures, the lot. All is good and life continues. Challenges do confront us and we tackle and face them as a team.

Birth Of A Daughter

A daughter may outgrow your lap, but she will never outgrow your heart.
Author Unknown

A good night of passion and I am pregnant again. This time I am having a girl. I cannot wait to dote on my little girl, to plait her hair and dress her in all things pink. I glow during my pregnancy, and I look the perfect picture of health. I even have men looking at me lustfully despite my little bump.

As the pregnancy progresses, the relationship takes another turn. The man is scarce again. He is distant and very cold. Any slight thing develops into an argument. This is weighing heavily on me and I feel I can't deal with it.

At every opportunity he puts me down and I feel like I am his enemy number one – the issue though is, I don't know why

I'm home from work this particular day and a bombshell is dropped with no care for the casualties. The issue has not been discussed and yet somehow a decision has been made. If this is a joke, it's a pretty lousy one and it is not funny because trust me I am not laughing. Believe it, Reader, he is serious. I am lost for words. *What on earth is going on in this man's head? Right now I wish I could get into his head and fix it up*. When I realise he is serious then I know this girl needs that old-time confidante, her mama. I have kept much away from her in order to protect her. This time I need my mama. Even my good friend, Teri, is not sufficient.

Lord, I cannot do this. I need strength from you. Help me deal with this, I pray in my heart. If my memory serves me well, this was the first time my prayer life changed. This prayer came from a broken, confused and scared place somewhere within me. This was no rushed rehearsed prayer. It came from the heart and the very core. When my son was born I thought I needed God, well I must have been kidding, I need him now to hold me together and let me feel him.

I hardly sleep all night. I toss and turn, coupled with the discomfort of being pregnant. What more am I expected to do now? Is this the time to call it a day? Honestly, right now I don't know, the only thing I know is that love hurts. I can go back to my parents, only I don't want to do that. As a society we have perfected the art of passing judgement. Nobody wants to be judged. I will be called names, and who wants to be called names?

I will be the laughing stock of the community. The one who could not bear the heat of marriage, the one who gave up at the very first appearance of a challenge, the one who has come home to her parents with two children. After all I have grown up being told marriage has never been plain sailing, and those that have celebrated milestone anniversaries also tell me it has never been easy but they have held on. So, my girlfriends, please don't judge me. I also want to conform to what society expects of me.

I need God to show up today and not tomorrow. I want Him to tell me what I need to do right now. No answer. Total silence. So what is the point of praying if He answers not? Trust me, many a time it feels like prayer is draining the very life out of me, but when I come to my senses and consider my options then I realise giving up praying is really not an option; prayer is my very lifeline.

Right now my life is like some Hollywood movie, only this is my life. He has just told me we are moving house. I imagine myself in a cramped room with a toddler and another on the way, with an occasional phone call to check how we are getting on.

'The final decision rests with you.' These are words from my loving mama when I finish pouring my heart out.

We finally move to a place we now call home a month before I'm due to give birth to my daughter. It's the 8th of July 1994, he is already home when I get back from visiting my mama. We barely exchange words and I get on with what I need to do. I'm due in four days. I'm saying this positively because this time I have a choice. I have decided to have a C-section. I am OK with it this time because it is my choice. I don't want to subject myself to seventeen hours of labour like the last time only to be cut open again. No. It's on my terms and I'm cool with it.

My son settles into bed and I stay up watching back-to-back episodes of *Friends*. I'm laughing along with Phoebe's stupidity. He comes back, having been out for a little drive and an argument ensues. For the life of me I can't tell you what it's about. I am heavily pregnant and not in any mood to argue.

'How about saying, Amanda I am leaving you?' I say to him in the middle of the argument. I stand up and go outside to stretch my legs and to calm myself down. It must be around 8 or 9 p.m.. I'm not sure. I walk around the yard and turn back. July is a cold, windy month. I go back, only to find I have been locked out. Frantic efforts to knock and get inside meet with no response.

'The Lord is my shepherd.' I recite the whole psalm as

I'm pacing up and down. I'm sure he is going to open the door at some point. 'Lord, if ever there is a time I have needed you to be my shepherd it is tonight. Keep me and my unborn child safe. Let me not go into labour tonight.' I waffle on and on at God. By now it is apparent that door will not be opened any time soon, if at all. 'Let your angels keep watch over us.' That night not a tear leaves my eye. I have to be strong for my unborn child. Today it's about survival. I am not breaking down, and hard as it is, no tear drops.

I manage to knock on the window of my home help's bedroom. Poor thing, she is wide awake. She opens the window with tears in her eyes. I reassure her I will be OK, but truthfully I don't know if I will. She manages to pass two small blankets through the window. I curl up on the back porch and try to be comfortable. The night is cold and long. I am scared and the baby kicks the entire night. I occasionally get up and walk, or stand to stretch my cramped legs and to ease my back.

I sing softly and quietly, to give me hope and to strengthen me. I recite Psalm 121 countless times. I know it's not in the right order. The order is insignificant right now. Someone recently said to me, 'Challenges are real. And so is God.' That I believe with my whole heart. I now know the true meaning of it. Call me an idiot, in fact call me whatever you want, I can tell you God is next to me and my unborn child this particular night.

You see, Reader, I could have died that night. My heart could have succumbed to the strain I was going through. There could have been burglars attempting to burgle the house and then alas find a woman to rape or kill. My baby could have died for reasons I cannot explain. I could have gone into labour with no soul to tender any help. Now tell me there was no divine intervention for my life that night.

Do you still need more reasons for me to prove God was with me? Why God allowed this I may not know but I sure want the chance to ask some day.

At the crack of dawn, he comes outside to use the adjoining bathroom. I look him straight in the eye and ask him how he has slept the entire night knowing I was outside with his unborn child? No answer.

I go in as he is using the bathroom and I crawl into my son's bed. My feet are frozen, in fact my entire body is a block of ice. My son is still asleep, oblivious of the drama that has been taking place. I try to keep warm next to him but I can't. A terrible headache grips me and my feet suddenly start swelling up. My body is telling me something is terribly wrong. I cannot feel any movement from the baby. I try to calm myself but fail. I'm increasingly aware that I'm seriously not well. The effects of last night are taking their toll. I make contact with my GP just to be on the safe side.

My doctor takes one good look at me and straight away she knows I am not a well woman. Only then do I break down. She lets me be. Right now I'm emotionally wrecked, drained, tired and the saddest woman you could ever come across. My blood pressure is dangerously high.

'How did you get here?' she inquires.

I don't have any strength to answer. We have a good doctor-patient relationship.

'You are not going back home. I am admitting you today.'

My blood pressure needs to be controlled. I get an injection straight away, and she arranges for my admission. She wants me to press charges against Alfred, but I refuse. That is not going to even up the score.

I am finally admitted to hospital and monitored every hour on the hour. Mama arrives as she learns I am in hospital. My home help has made contact with her. She does not ask me any questions, neither does she expect me to explain. She wants me to be well.

The 12th of July 1994 heralds the birth of my gorgeous princess. I am prepared for theatre, and before I know it I am out for the count.

I wake up from my state of unconsciousness before the doctor has finished stitching me up. I want to scream but I can't. I can hear the medical team talking. In goes the needle and I feel the pain. I must have flinched or something, and it is then the medical team realise the anaesthetic has worn off. One of them holds my hands while the doctor continues to stitch me up. That was painful. Even to this day when I go back to that memory I can still feel that pain.

The nurses place my baby on my chest and put my hands around her. I am wheeled to the recovery room. Ten minutes later I feel so cold and I ask for extra blankets. Still I'm not warming up. A portable heater is brought to the room, and slowly and gradually I start to recover.

She is such a beautiful baby with lots of hair, and a very strong set of lungs. One of the nurses says, 'She is going to be a good singer.' And would you believe it, she has one amazing voice and is indeed a good singer.

Once again Mama comes to the rescue. She nurses me and my baby girl. She is full of joy as she fulfils her motherly and grandmotherly responsibilities and she takes them seriously.

My children are my world and they keep me going. All my energies are channelled towards them and I am determined to do all within my power to give them the best. I might as well resign myself to being a single mum. The difference is I am under the same roof as their dad.

He seems to be having a good time and it's apparent

there is now another woman on the scene. As it turns out his mistress is also a teacher, at a neighbouring school to mine. I get snippets of information: she is not a fully qualified teacher and is much older than I am.

I thought men who cheat normally go for younger women to make the other half more jealous. *I'm thinking you could have done better than that, Alfred.* As is normally the case, the wife is the last to know. Some of my work colleagues know her.

We co-exist, and I still in my foolish way hope that one day things might change. Countless prayers are said in the hope of reviving my marriage. The more I pray the worse the situation becomes.

Loose, Dangerous Words

*'Words are like eggs dropped from great heights; you can
no more call them back than ignore the mess they leave
when they fall'.*
Jodi Picoult

It's another normal school day. We have just finished
assembly and the headmaster calls a brief catch-up
meeting with the teachers. Our Early Years department is
in need of a few resources which I let him know about in
the hearing of all my colleagues.

'Go and ask the MDC.' To say I am shocked would be an
understatement. I simply don't know what to make of that.
The other teachers look just as puzzled.

'This old man is treading on dangerous ground,' I tell
myself. I settle the children, give them some work and
head straight to the office – this is the same headmaster
who a few years back did not appraise me for a pay rise
because I turned down his sexual advances.

'Please can you explain what your statement meant?' I
challenge him.

'I meant exactly what I said,' he says with such
arrogance.

'Whatever my political affiliation, it has nothing to do
with the school or with you personally!' I roar.

'Why don't you just leave the school then?'

'This is not your school and I will leave when I want to!' I rant and rave and by now I just want to gouge out his privates. 'Get it into your thick, old head, I will never sleep with you, not even if my life depended on it!' The man is old, wrinkly and is the new definition of the word ugly. I stand up, bang the door and leave his office.

This is not a stance to be taken likely. The time is not a safe period for civil servants in Zimbabwe. Civil servants, teachers included, are associated with the new movement daring to stand up to the Mugabe regime, the MDC (Movement for Democratic Change), and viewed as having the potential to influence their communities against the ruling party. The dilemma is I can't report this to any authorities. Reporting will bring attention to myself. The solace, I guess, is that none of my colleagues are favourites of the ruling party, so I know I'm 'safe'.

Wednesday Afternoon Miracle

*'Miracles happen every day, change your perception of
what a miracle is and you'll see them all around you'.*
Jon Bon Jovi

I wear the mask perfectly well. If no one tells you, you
won't know that I am a broken person. I am tired of
praying. God is too silent for my liking. I don't know how
to stay in this dead and emotionally abusive relationship
and I don't know how to get out of it either. I make life as
normal as I can for my children. What scares me is I know
that I am slowly getting past caring and loving. The line
that separates love and hate is wearing thin. My love is
slowly being chipped away and that concerns me.

The urge to find out about the other woman is so great,
but my pride prevents me from sinking low. Why should I
have issues with her? She has been approached and an
undying love declared to her. Trust me, girlfriend, it hurts
knowing someone has been chosen over you. If I say it
does not hurt, then I am a damn liar. It kills me inside. I
start analysing myself and my inadequacies. None
warrants this type of treatment. Now I find I only need
enough strength for each day.

School is over, and I decide to visit my mama. It's a
beautiful Wednesday afternoon. As I am waiting for the
bus another person comes towards the stop. We are a few
yards from each other. Strangely enough something starts

happening to me. My heart suddenly beats so fast I can see my chest moving. I get my water bottle out and I have a sip. I feel like I am about to pass out. *At least I have lovely matching underwear in case I pass out*, I attempt to make light of what I am currently feeling.

I hear a voice as clear as crystal saying, *That is Alfred's mistress*. I look around to see who on earth is playing such a sick joke. There is not a soul around apart from this other total stranger waiting for the bus. Maybe I'm going cuckoo in my head. I'm not hallucinating nor am I drunk. But someone has spoken to me loud and clear. I remain composed and then I notice this person is looking at me very suspiciously. Our eyes meet and she quickly looks away.

Thank you, Lord. Right, girls, what does one do with such information? There is the enemy, right in front of me. The Lord has delivered her right on to my turf and surely I can do as I please. The more I look at her the more I can sense she is not herself. Her behaviour confirms the message that has just been relayed to me. The temptation to cause a scene and tell the world that she is a husband snatcher is so great. I want to rip her to shreds and shout all the obscenities under the sun.

Just as my mouth is getting ready to hurl the insults, as the first word is about to leave my lips, just as I am about to deliver my own justice I am hit with the thought, *The battle is not yours but mine declares the Lord. Vengeance is mine.*

No, no, Lord. Just step aside and let me deal with this woman once and for all. I battle with this for a while, and God is just not giving in to my demands. This is not fair.

The bus comes and we both get on board. She sits a couple of seats in front of me. I remain calm. If you think staying calm is easy, then you really don't get it. I am in a constant fight with the voice of reason telling me to remain calm and the urge to do justice getting even greater. I know that if I start my barrage of insults to her, every person in the bus would be on my side, after all I am the 'scorned wife'. Trust me, Reader, I need not lay a finger on her; the public, especially any married women that might be on the bus, will show solidarity.

She would be stripped naked; I mean literally stripped naked. Hollywood would come alive inside this bus. *If only you could just allow me to have my own way, Lord.* By this time, I want to jump on her and cause untold damage. Someone and something holds me back at that precise point, and I am constantly being pushed back to my seat. And yet I cannot let her walk free. That is how I am thinking at the time.

'Lord if that was your voice I heard, I don't understand why but thanks anyway,' I whisper, rather angry for not being allowed to have my own way.

It turns out the voice is spot on. The woman in the bus is indeed my husband's mistress. I struggle with the knowledge I now possess. Her face keeps coming into my memory as though to haunt me. I want to approach her and challenge her but a voice keeps saying no to me, so I oblige and let her go scot free.

Alfred and I are two separate individuals living under the same roof. He is living his own life and I am living mine.

My encounter with his girlfriend is obviously discussed between the two of them. I am made aware of this through a conversation I have with him. He seems surprised that I have remained calm even after knowing about his girlfriend. He has been expecting a reaction from me, and I don't give him any. I still have a bit of pride and self-preservation, and besides, right now I don't have the strength to fight and I don't want to fight.

What he fails to realise is that my love is waxing cold. I don't hate him, far from it, but right now he is not worth me making a spectacle of myself. The pain and the humiliation is so great I am not putting myself through any unnecessary pain. It would have been a perfectly normal thing to react.

You see, Reader, when you get put down a lot, you become immune, all you want is a little semblance of normality in your life. I have an issue with fighting and making trouble with the 'other woman'. The real culprit is the man. A grown man who vowed for better and for worse, promised to love only me, that is the person to deal with. Never fight the mistress. If she is stupid enough to think she is better than me, the wife, shame on her. More often than not, she will taste the bitterness of her own medicine in due season. One's sins always have a way of finding one out.

Perpetrators of any form of abuse feel threatened when they do not get a reaction that proves to them they have a hold over the victim and at the same time, I do not want those around me to loathe him either. The latter is a characteristic of victims of any form of abuse.

It has been said *sticks and stones can break my bones but words can never hurt me*. How far from the truth that is!

Falling Apart

"I find so many opportunities to fall, to falter, and fail when I refuse to surrender to change. Change will come into my room and rearrange my tidy world. Then like dominoes, one thing changed falls upon another until it feels like the world is collapsing around me. But when I yield, when I surrender to the necessary change, I can stand back and look at the beautiful picture created by what seemed to be my world falling apart."
Stella Payton

1995, and I'm still alive. Alive because breath is still being granted to me, but dead as far as my soul is concerned. I need an escape, something to make me feel human, normal and a woman. I start to self-harm, only it's not the physical kind that we all think of or know.

Retail therapy becomes my way of coping. I spend money like there is no tomorrow. My kids are clad in everything designer. There is not a hair out of place. I don't know the meaning of a bad hair day. The truth is all this is just camouflage. I feel I am in control, and the truth is, I'm not.

Financial problems spiral out of control. Before I realise, I am in serious debt. I don't know how to stop. I am even getting money from moneylenders. I feel a million dollars when people admire and comment on how well dressed my children are. I want to prove to Alfred that I am still standing. It's only when the the moneylenders threaten to come and get my furniture that I get a reality check. It is painful, embarrassing. A hard and a long road, and I endeavour to get out of that situation. After hard work, living on the breadline and forgoing so much, I finally get there. I'm debt free. There is a serious self-discipline needed to overcome such a habit. It is an addiction of its own kind. Even as I search the scriptures, God has told me how He feels about being in debt, so I am thankful to God for helping me through this.

I look back now and realise that before most traumatic events take place in my life, God always prepares me or makes it known to me before it actually happens. I love reading and keeping up with current affairs. In fact, both Alfred and I love reading two of our local papers.

It's a Thursday afternoon and he is already home by the time I arrive. Pleasantries are exchanged, I spend a little time with the children and then get on with my marking. I completely forget about the newspaper that day.

It's now Sunday afternoon. The kids are playing and I am relaxing. I decide to go through all the papers for that week. I look through the business section of one particular paper.

What on earth? My house is advertised for sale in the local paper! Please tell me this is a dream and I will soon wake up from it. Somebody please shake me as violently as you can and wake me up from this nightmare.

This is not a dream, it's real. I snap myself out of the shock and horror of this discovery. Where is that voice of reason when I need it? This Sunday is the longest day of my life. Where is the voice of reason? It appears when I would rather it does not and when I need it, it's not there. These are my thoughts. Keep calm and carry on. Let anyone tell me that such calmness is humanly possible, I will disagree and will look you straight in the eye and tell you it is humanly impossible. How can you be rational when all around you is falling apart? If not God, then who? Please, somebody tell me.

Call me a fool, stupid or anything you wish, I am not. I am tired and scared of being strong. Now I want the whole world to see that I am vulnerable just like the rest of them. I want the world to know that I, too, can crumble. I want someone to realise that I am inadequate. That is what makes us human, isn't it? After all who says being weak is wrong?

It would appear the Lord above thinks otherwise. He gives me more strength, the very thing I don't want right now. Without saying a word, I block the sale of the house and continue as though nothing has happened. People come to view the house in my presence. I look and say not a word. Wow; life, when you think you have sussed it out, presents in a different formula.

As usual, on this particular Sabbath morning I get myself and the kids ready to go to church. He offers to take us to church. The kids enjoy the rides in their dad's car, so I am not going to deny them that one luxury.

Church is over and I walk back home with the children. My son is reciting his new Bible verse for me, my daughter comfortably strapped to my back, and we look picture perfect. As we approach home, I get my keys ready. By now we are standing outside our gate and I notice something unusual. It appears as though we have been burgled.

I open the gate and we go in. It's not a break in, it is a break out. Someone has finally moved out.

Again an unusual calm washes over me. I fight back my tears. I fix lunch and feed the kids. Kennedy asks a few questions for which I don't have answers. My daughter is too young to say anything, but clever enough to notice something is wrong.

Monday comes and it's back to work as normal. A week goes by and not a word from Alfred. Each time a car drives close by our gate my daughter opens her big eyes as she thinks it's Daddy. That alone crushes me. At the realisation it's not 'Dada', her face falls with disappointment, and she crawls back into my hands. What do you say to a three-year-old and an eighteen-month-old girl expecting Dad to walk in at any minute? You just love them even more.

I'm on a long road to nowhere and I pray this prayer: *Lord, I don't know what you expect of me but I cannot do this anymore. Marriage is honourable in your eyes but unfortunately there is nothing honourable about mine. This marriage has been over for a long time. Please let me accept it and let me have the strength to do something about it.* I walk back home, feeling much better for the words I have uttered more to myself than to God.

A week after that walk I approach a lawyer and file for a divorce. My mind is made up. Nobody in heaven or on earth can make me change my mind. Not even the voice of reason. I am done. This is about love; love that has been abused and taken advantage of. I have been betrayed and surely I am justified. Please don't berate me with the God-hates-divorce line. Would you say the same if you were in my place? Does God endorse abuse of a spouse and children? No I don't think so.

Do I hate him now that I want to divorce him? Far from it. This is God's honest truth. My heart has been broken and it cannot be broken any more, for to allow it to continue being broken is to agree to die. Hate is a very strong word, and is one emotion I cannot afford to entertain. All I want now is to let go while I still care for him. I am running away from hating him. I don't want to, so please do understand me.

I ask myself numerous countless questions, unfortunately the answers are not as clear cut as I would like them to be. Is this life a reflection of how much I have valued myself as an individual? Do I see myself as someone who is of value or am I receiving what I have invested in my own value? Could it be that I have lost the sense of who I am or want to be? After all, God says I am fearfully and wonderfully made. From this point on I want this to be my mantra.

Till Death Do Us Part

*Death leaves a heartache no one can heal, love leaves a
memory no one can steal.*
Richard Puz

The divorce never happens, and I can't tell you why,
because I don't know either. Somehow the papers get
mixed up in the post. Another set is sent out and
mysteriously nothing happens. When the papers finally get
delivered again there is no action. I stop bothering, after
all the marriage ended before it even began. A piece of
paper appears insignificant now; it's what I feel in my
heart and the facts that make the difference.

I continue my life and it's as 'normal' as it can be, being
the result of a higher power taking charge. How I can still
wake up and face the dawning of a new day, how I manage
to get dressed and go to work and stand in front of a class.
How I can still afford to smile and have faith in mankind,
it can only be God.

It's the 19th of April 1996 around 7 p.m. My neighbour is
trying to get my attention. She tells me there are
policemen outside my gate and that they have been
knocking for a considerable length of time. My gate is a bit
of a distance from the house so it can be tricky sometimes
to immediately pick up on the presence of visitors.

I go outside to attend to the police. I have my keys in my
hands but I don't open my gate right away. Realising I'm

not keen, they ask to be let in. The kids are already in bed and not aware of their presence.

The policemen start to ask questions concerning Alfred. The line of questioning is rather humiliating as I have to explain that he no longer resides with us. I am asked to prove that I am his wife. That I struggle with. Technically and on paper I'm still his wife but in reality I am not. I try to resist that request.

They insist and I decide to turn the tables and I am the one asking questions now. The sad part is they appear to have some sort of attitude towards me and I don't know why. It could be because I am a woman; some of these people have little or no respect for women anyway, or there is something they know that I don't.

Realising I am not going to be intimidated, they work on the assumption that I am the wife. The questioning continues. I also intensify my line of questioning and realise they are not forthcoming with their answers. At some point they will have to tell me; they can't just drive up to my house and ask me all these questions. I know there is mismanagement of time and resources within some government departments, but not in such a stupid way. So I wait. It could be worse, I tell myself.

'Your husband was found dead this afternoon. It appears he committed suicide.'

Nothing on God's earth could have prepared me for this. How do you prepare for it? My whole body goes into a violent convulsion. I am sweating and shaking uncontrollably. Suddenly there is not enough oxygen in the room, I'm hyperventilating.

The next thing I remember, one of the police officers is handing me a glass of water and trying to sit me up. I gain some composure, and my mind goes back to what the officers are saying to me. It can't be true, maybe they have made a mistake.

I head to my children's bedroom; they are sleeping peacefully. I hug them and sob. Tears flow as though a tap has been turned on. The officers give me space and let me have that moment. I hold on to my children, I don't want to let go of them.

It's as though I am abruptly reminded of my marriage vows. Did they really have to come so true so quickly and did it have to be this way? Is this level of pain what I signed up for? I need answers. I want the ground to open up and swallow me. What have I done to deserve all this? Does life have to be this hard? Well, Reader, I wish I had clear cut answers.

This is the darkest day of our lives. I am only thirty at the time. I am at the prime of my life and my status in society has changed within minutes. I have two young children, both under five. How do I come through the other side?

The police require that I come and identify the body. I ask them if it has to be done immediately. Unfortunately, the answer is yes. One of them drops yet another bombshell. They have his body in their van parked outside my house. *Oh no, Lord, this is downright cruel. I have never heard of anything like it in my life.* Obviously life is having a good time torturing me. My distress is incomprehensible. I can't go through this all by myself. I need my mama with me.

Thank God for parents. They lay down their lives for their children and they go the extra mile. They comfort, they feel their pain and they share in their joys. They encourage when experiencing disappointments. They might not be as educated as I am, they might not be 'cool enough', but trust me, they have my back. There are no words to describe them. Nothing is too big where their children are concerned. They lay their lives down for them.

Cherish yours if you still have the opportunity.

The man I loved, the man I had vowed to love till death did us part is now lying inside a coffin. *Why me*? I ask that question over and over to the point of self-destruction.

And why not you? I hear my mother's voice in my head. Apparently a strong woman never asks why, but she asks for strength to come through the other side. Right now, I need that strength.

The alarm is raised and family and friends converge to my home to comfort and support. Mother-in-law and his brothers and uncles are present too. There is tension between them and me, and I'm not sure why. If anything, I think we should be holding each other's hands for strength. They are not being cooperative, and we can move forward and bury our dead. They tell me they suspect foul play, and as for their number one suspect, well you have guessed correctly, it's me.

Imagine that. For starters the man moved out on me and left, and I hadn't the slightest knowledge of his whereabouts. Only now I know he is in the morgue, and I don't take any pleasure in that.

Their behaviour is appalling. At some point there is a bitter exchange of words. Right now I'm not seeing any justice in the world. What have I done to deserve this? You see, Reader, there are some cultures who believe if a man (husband) dies, then the woman has killed him so she can claim his inheritance.

In the heat of the moment, when their behaviour is really tearing me down, I get the strength to defend myself and put these people in their rightful place. Again that voice nags and beckons me to be silent and do that which is right. I am thinking to myself, what benefit have I derived from doing 'that which is right' so far? Heartache and more heartache and humiliation.

I do what is right by my children and by the conviction of my conscience. I go ahead and plan the funeral. It's a pretty decent one, considering. He is the father of my children and the man I vowed to love 'till death do us part'.

It's now a couple of months after the funeral and I am having one of my power walks. I am pouring my heart and soul out. *Lord I am only thirty years old and I have two very young children to take care of. How will I get by all by myself? The world is judging me right now and I don't know how to do this.*

Like a flash of lightning, I am reminded that I have been on my own for a while now so nothing is really different, the only thing is that I am officially a widow. This is my official status from henceforth. Aren't widows supposed to be old women, not someone who is thirty? Should I not be enjoying life instead of mourning a dead spouse?

How does this work, Reader? I am now declared a widow, yet Mama is still a married woman. Where is the justice in that? Please don't misunderstand me. I am not wishing my father to have been the one dead here. I love the man, but my point is, wouldn't it be more acceptable if it was the other way round? Each official form that I have to complete where I am required to state my marital status, I have to state 'widow', there is no denying it. Like it or hate it, that's the truth staring me in the face.

I pray and hope the world sees beyond my new label. I hope I am not referred to as that young widow. I want people to know me for who I am. I hope no one sees me as an object of pity. In fact, world, do not sympathise but empathise if you understand my circumstances. I pray that there is not a man who now sees me as being in desperate need of a new husband.

Others will say, she has a bit on the side who is keeping her 'alive'. I hope you catch my drift, Reader. After all, as far as they are concerned I am free to do whatever I will.

All this scares me. I hope when I speak to any man, or when a man speaks to me, no woman feels threatened or thinks I am up to no good. You see labels come with assumptions. My every action and word will now be brought to question. I am under no illusion, but the truth of the matter is I am who I am and I hope the world continues to see me as one of them.

The months that follow are very trying. Knowing he is gone forever is hard to comprehend. I am angry because I think Alfred has taken a coward's way out, but on the other hand who am I to judge his motive and what really drove him to that? You see I am angry; my children are without a father. I am angry my daughter is never going to enjoy the special relationship that exists between father and daughter, angry my son will never have a father figure to put him right and answer his questions. To them Daddy is now just a picture on the mantelpiece.

God, how can you say you really care? I don't understand. Barrel-loads of tears cover my path and I almost stumble and fall for lack of seeing my path. A hug, a tight squeeze, a word of comfort and that much needed silence when there are no words. My faith in the human race is once again restored. We all have a little measure of kindness and when required to share it, people do share.

When you need to show kindness please don't make the person in need explain themselves and relive the painful experience. Extend a human touch, it goes a long way, and you will never understand unless you have been on the receiving end.

I don't know how we measure sorrow or heartache. Is it by the show of tears or by facial expressions? Is it by resigning ourselves from society? The truth of the matter is we cannot measure, though the onlooker may think so. To the one hurting, these don't even begin to scratch the surface. My sorrow is beyond words. I am empty inside.

To Forgive Is Divine

It's not an easy journey, to get to a place where you forgive people. But it is such a powerful place, because it frees you
Tyler Perry

Healing has to happen. If I continue lying in this sick bed, then I am going to die. I want to live for my children. They need their mama in good and sound mind. I know I am angry and hurting right now. I tell myself that nothing I could have done or said would have made any difference. Alfred should have learned to be a different man for himself first and then for those around him.

I accept I am not to blame, so I stop blaming myself. I'm sure if a friend came to me and told me all the things that happened to me were happening to them, I would have been able to tell them what to do in that situation. I would have thought they were foolish and insane to have put up with it. I would have signposted them to organisations that would have offered them help. I would have taken the drastic step of getting them out myself if it were possible, and yet I could not do the same for myself. When asked by a friend if I hold any malice towards the mistress, I tell them not at all, and that is God's honest truth.

The mistress makes efforts to have an audience with me. Firstly, I refuse. *Over my dead body. It's not happening.* As I yearn so much to discharge myself from this sick bed,

I soon realise I might have to do things I would prefer not to do. Even my wise, all-knowing Mama wouldn't encourage this audience. *Don't judge her.* Which parent wouldn't be bitter towards those that hurt their children? After careful consideration I decide to see her. I tell not a soul about my intentions.

A few minutes before our appointment, I want to leave. After all, I have nothing to say to her. As I prepare to walk away, something tells me to hear her out. Really, hear her out. I don't want to, but if I want to heal, forgive and move on I need to do it. I know I am not going to suddenly become her best buddy, she can deal with her conscience. I am not seeking any reconciliation, I want to free myself and move my life on the best I can.

Let it be known that forgiveness doesn't necessarily mean reconciliation. This case is one of those.

I meet her in town. She is visibly nervous and shaken, poor thing. She extends her hand to give me a handshake. No response from me. I can't bring myself to do that. It would be hypocritical of me; yes I need to heal, but offering her a hand is far too much right now. Maybe in time, who knows? I am no saint and I am not going to pretend to be one. I sit and wait for her story.

She starts with an apology. I don't know what she is apologising for. She pours her heart and soul out. She sobs and sniffles, tears and mucus together. I reach for my bag and silently hand her some tissues. I am not sure why I do that. Is it because I am feeling her pain or is it because her snot is disgusting? Then I realise that I am still 100 per cent human. She goes to lengths in narrating how she had discovered Alfred hanging in her house and raising the alarm and all the rest of it. Well, that is a picture that will haunt her for the rest of her life.

Even at this point her sobbing is a bit confusing to me.

Should it not be me sobbing here, I wonder. As she continues with her pitiful sobbing a silly thought crosses my mind. Is she sobbing because Alfred has gone to the grave with his 'willie'? A little rebuke by a form of a thought comes to my mind and I change my attitude and remember the reason I'm doing this. It's for me and not her.

She asks me if I got the suicide note that Alfred left. I didn't answer her. She was not here to ask me any questions, if anything I should be doing the asking. Of course I had been given the note by the police and what was it to her anyway? My contribution to this one-sided conversation are words to this effect: 'The only victims in all this are my two children who now don't have a father. I hope you find peace. As for me, I will rise and I will survive.'

I stand up and leave. When I get back home, I spend most of the evening cuddling my kids and seeing the best part of Alfred in them. It is that best of him I had so much wanted to love unconditionally. Yes these two are the best of him.

A Shoulder To Lean On

Our brothers and sisters are there with us from the dawn of our personal stories to the inevitable dusk
Susan Scarf Merrell

Life has to go on and I can't die with the dead. There are two souls that need me to brush up, pick myself up, and continue in life's race. I have good days and bad days. Like everybody else I will do my best. If my best isn't good enough, then I really don't know. I have to rise from the ashes, as it were. Rise I will.

I have the support of a brother, the second eldest. He becomes the glue that holds me together. He is an intelligent, kind man. He promises his undying support for me and the children, and he lives up to his promise. He takes them under his wing and is proud to be their uncle. Family is his number one priority.

I'm confident that my son has bagged himself a top-notch role model in his uncle. I know his uncle will have that 'man to man' talk when it's needed. I know he will restore Kenny's confidence in humanity and male folk in general. Every cloud has a silver lining, I comfort myself. The bond between uncle, nephew and niece is strong and good.

It's towards the end of 1996, and 'Uncle Gri', as he is affectionately known, suffers a bout of ill health. We are all hopeful of a recovery. The bond between him and my children is just enviable. I dare not discipline them when he is around. He doesn't spoil them; he is just being their uncle. Christmas of 1996 comes and goes. After Christmas he takes a turn for the worse.

He is in and out of hospital. His health deteriorates, and the family decides it is best to look after him at home. Systems are put in place to best care for him.

It's now the New Year of 1997. Watching his face light up when Nonky and Kenny are by his side is such a comfort. They are children and not aware that death is staring them in the face. I have been down this road before and I can't lose my brother as well.

Ten months after Alfred's death, my brother breathes his last. The phone call comes via the headmaster's office. I am in class, and suddenly I am summoned to the office to receive a call from home. The news is broken to me. I sigh and shake my head. The deputy head offers to take me home.

Kenny is at nursery and Nonky is home. I take one look at my daughter and only then do the tears come. We lay my brother to rest.

Months after, one thing is very evident: my son is angry and confused. He is only five and has lost his uncle, his super hero. A few months after losing my brother, I visit a friend with my children. Dinner is served and Kennedy is asked to say grace. He starts crying.

'I hate God.' There is silence in the room. 'Why did he take my uncle?'

I reach out, and hold him close to me. What we need now is silence. There is no need to fill the room with words, in fact what can I say to my son right now?

Bricks & Mortar

A house is made of walls and beams; a home is built with love and dreams.
Author Unknown

Institutions and people are becoming more corrupt in Zimbabwe than ever before. People's morals are at point zero. It's all about who you know and how much money you have. Those with money, or know people in high places, call the shots. Bribes are part of everyday life. Those who are meant to uphold the rule of law frequently violate it instead.

I am sorting things out as far as Alfred's estate is concerned. Another bombshell: it appears money changed hands regarding the blocked sale of the house. It emerges both Alfred and the 'buyer' were reliably informed that unless I consented to sell, the house could not be sold and any attempt to do so would be illegal. Bingo, the case is mine to win.

The case goes backwards and forwards. The lawyer's costs spiral out of control but I am determined. I fight tooth and nail to keep my home. Soon it turns nasty. It becomes an issue of who knows who, rather than truth and justice. This goes on for over two years.

I am getting tired and worn out. My fighting spirit is gradually wearing thin. The weakness I once longed for is slowly engulfing me. The more I fight against the house sale, the more I feel like I'm being controlled from beyond the grave. The more I commit the issue to God, the more deafening is God's silence.

I go power walking. Remember this has a different meaning for me. It is not for physical fitness; it is for spiritual fitness. You see when I go power walking, I disconnect from the hustle and bustle of the world. I create this sacred place and I am me. I remove all masks and get real with God. It would appear as though God is reminding me that the healing journey I have embarked on will not be easy and what has just been impressed in my mind has to be part of the process. How does a mother, a woman, and by the way a widow, comprehend this? I refuse to accept defeat and I try one last time. Considerable time elapses. I need to make a decision.

Another day, another power walk. It's Sunday morning. I stand outside the house. I talk to myself for a considerable length of time.

'Yes, Lord, this is only bricks and mortar. My healing journey is more important than bricks and mortar. Yes, I have children who need a roof over their heads. Yes, they need a place to call home, but this is definitely not it. My job is secure and I *will* secure a home for my children, not by might but I am certain I am going to do it. Watch this space. Holding on to this one means I would be willing to continue living in the past. If I want to heal, I need to be willing to lose it all. The past is not holding me captive any more. It's my future that matters now. Memories of the past may be carried over to my future, that's fine, but my past will not define my future.'

Future, Here I Come

Life is divided into three terms – that which was, which is, and which will be. Let us learn from the past to profit by the present, and from the present, to live better in the future.
William Wordsworth

Satisfied everything has been packed and moved, I take the house keys to my lawyer and instruct him to stop pursuing the issue of the house. He wonders why I am giving up. Life is important now. My state of mind, my physical health, all of me needs to be on point for the sake of my kids. Show me anyone who has enjoyed luxuries beyond the grave – zilch. When it comes to material things or money, they all cease to matter when life itself is threatened. Life is the ultimate and today I choose life. This girl is not fighting losing battles anymore.

If walking away from this property proves that I have a chink in my strong armour, so let it be known, I do have a chink.

We all heal at varying levels and at different rates. Nothing beats life experiences. I pray that each woman, man, boy or girl reading this will find peace within their soul as they recover from life's challenges. I don't know who your voice of reason is, I don't know who you call on when times are dark, I don't know who has been a constant feature in your life, but one thing I do know: God has been the constant in mine. You might not want to believe in my God, but that's cool: after all we live in a free world. All I can say is try Him and find out for yourself.

It has been said, 'Death is not the greatest loss in life. Loss is when life dies inside you while you are still alive,' so you see why I'm refusing to 'die' just yet.

You really think life would have had enough of me by now? You are kidding, right? Keep on reading.

Heathrow Airport – December 2001

When someone you love dies, you are given the gift of "second chances". Their eulogy is a reminder that the living can turn their lives around at any point. You're not bound by the past; that is who you used to be. You're reminded that your feelings are not who you are, but how you felt at that moment. Your bad choices defined you yesterday, but they are not who you are today. Your future doesn't have to travel the same path with the same people. You can start over.
Shannon L. Alder

I have been granted a six-month visitor's visa. *Someone please pinch me.* I will keep my head down, and I'm positive the regime of the day will soon be out of power in my country, and Zimbabwe will be back on its feet. There will be no more civil unrest, no more unlawful arrests and senseless killings. I will huddle with my fellow Zimbabweans in the meantime, and we will hope and pray 'home' gets back to normality.

At the earliest opportunity I make contact with my sister and tell her I have landed. This is a journey that I have not charted before. I am in a foreign country and in no way sure how long it will be for, and I don't know how things will turn out. I had to make the decision to leave the children behind. I don't want to unsettle them to dangers I know nothing of myself. It is no easy decision, and yet I have to make it. By faith I trust my sister as she steps into my shoes; after all, we all hope things will settle down in Zimbabwe and I will soon be back home. She is the legal guardian for my children while I'm away, and, oh boy, does she do a marvellous job. I owe you one, Little Sis.

Slowly I settle into a foreign routine and I familiarise myself with my immediate surroundings. Time moves on, and there are still no signs of immediate changes in Zimbabwe. The situation is getting worse by the day. I have to make big decisions. Two months have gone already and I am expected back home.

To make my flight as safe as possible and not raise any suspicions I requested a two-month leave of absence from the Ministry of Education in Zimbabwe. My coming to the UK is not public knowledge; as far as most people are concerned, I am in Zimbabwe.

Right now, my career in teaching will be ending, and who cares anyway when I am constantly looking over my shoulders? When I can be suspected of turning the children against the government of the day? The truth is that right now I don't know when I will be going home, and I guess I just have to wait and see.

Reality strikes; it's not going to be a bed of roses here either. At least there are no bloody protests, or the political unrest that rules Zimbabwe. That is a consolation. My visa does not allow me to work, neither am I entitled to any public funds. So I need to think about how to survive, and of course my widow status means I am the sole provider for my children.

Soon I realise I am not the only Zimbabwean in this situation. We either work as illegal immigrants or live on handouts. The concept of employment agencies is new to me and I enrol with one. Right now I am willing to do anything, I mean anything, to survive and provide for my two. I know that I am playing Russian roulette with my life but so be it, I have chosen survival, and survival it will be.

I am learning new things every day. I am put through various training courses and do what I'm expected to do to the best of my ability. I acquire new skills and I develop myself at any given opportunity. I am building a social and support network within my local church community, and I meet more acquaintances from back home.

I have training on this particular Thursday, which will last until 4 p.m. A friend has asked me to come and mind her children for a short while before her husband gets home. I agree. Unfortunately, the training goes beyond 4 p.m. After training I go straight home and decide I will see my friend in the morning. It's the following morning before I go and visit my friend. She is a bit offish with me; she is not her usual self. I feel uncomfortable and I pluck up courage and ask her what is bothering her.

She tells me they had to deal with the police yesterday evening regarding the children. The conclusion they came to is that someone called the police and reported that their children had been left on their own when their shift times crossed over. I am shocked. Now work it out, Reader, I was meant to babysit last night, I didn't turn up for whatever reason, and then the next thing my friends are dealing with the police. Who is the prime suspect as informant here?

Once their suspicions are made known to me it makes me so sad. Have you ever been in a situation where you begin to doubt your own innocence? That is what is going on inside of me. I don't know how to prove my case. I cling on to the hope that one day the truth will come out.

Two weeks later, the truth does come out. A meeting has been arranged between them and Social Services. It is then it comes to light that their eldest child (aged maybe five or

117

six at the time) had picked up the phone and dialled 999, and when he heard a voice on the other end of the phone he must have panicked and put the receiver down. Apparently the baby was crying in the background. The call was traced and that is how the police ended up at their place. We kiss and make up. This is the true essence of life. It has its weird ways. One has to laugh at how it manifests itself, but most of all learn great lessons.

I enrol at a college and they will be taking care of my visa from now on.

A couple of years later, I find myself in a similar situation, again with the same friends. Humans are creatures of habit. I have one particular place and bench that I sit when I am in church. Very close friends sit with me. We have been sitting there every week since I arrived.

I am one of the first ones in church and I go straight to 'my place', where I know my dear friends will be joining me soon. After a while, I see them walk in, I shuffle along in acknowledgement, only this time they don't come over to me, although there is more than enough room. They sit two benches behind me. OK, maybe not a big deal, I tell myself.

We commence our lesson study as usual. My friend's husband is rather vocal today; he loves a good debate and is a very good participant in discussions, and he keeps them lively. As the study continues, it is apparent he is angry and his comments are directed to someone, but whom? It's making me feel uncomfortable, and I don't know why. As time goes by, it becomes clear that his comments are directed at me.

Church is over, and I approach the wife, tell her I can feel there is something wrong and ask if we can try and solve the problem. She acknowledges there is an issue and she promises she will call me on Monday.

Monday comes and goes and no phone call comes my way.

On Tuesday I make the call myself. The long and short of the story is that some gossip has allegedly taken place between our local pastor at the time and myself about them. To say I am shocked, Reader, is an understatement. I don't know how to take this or deal with it. These people are my friends, in fact I see them as family. I don't want to fall out. I resolve to get to the bottom of this, and if it means I have wronged my friends, let it be known. I am not too big to own up. She is not giving me much information, so I guess I have to talk to the pastor and find out what it is that I have supposedly done.

I battle with the idea of approaching him. For starters, what am I going to say to him and how do I approach him? This is the pastor, not my peer. I commit this to serious prayer, then I approach my adopted daddy, Jarrett, for counsel. He advises I should approach the pastor.

I go to see him on a Wednesday evening before the prayer meeting. I relay the events of the previous week and what has been said, asking why they thought we had discussed this other family.

The pastor tells me that a certain member had approached him over concerns that confidential information regarding people's way of tithing was being leaked, so he had approached the friend's husband over these concerns in an attempt to keep things confidential.

So why associate me with this? The penny drops: one of them is the local church treasurer. In one of our discussions about the goodness of the Lord we discussed the importance of tithing. I expressed concerns over a family member's lack of tithing or my suspicions. So I spoke to my friends and asked them to enlighten the family member on the benefits of tithing.

So now they have linked this back to me. The pastor assures me this has nothing to do with me and that I should stop worrying about it. I remain as civil as I can, but unfortunately my friendship with these people is cracked. I am positive, though, that one day it will mend and those cracks will be smoothed.

Have you ever been in a position where people have judged or wrongly accused you? It can be crippling and it eats away at your confidence. When you look deep within, we judge each other based on the standards we have or the lack of them. Sometimes it is borne out of emotions and feelings of jealousy. In this instance I'm not sure what motivates it.

New Life, New Dreams

Never be afraid to trust an unknown future to a known
God
Corrie ten Boom

The church community is now my close family. I make new friends, and a family that adopts me as their own. I call them my UK mum and dad. Zimbabwe continues to experience political unrest, and the economic situation hits rock bottom. I speak to my family as often as possible and offer financial support as much as I can. I still need to obtain a recognised status in the UK, but my youngest brother, affectionately known as MK, has been able to come over to Britain. I am happy, there is someone here who shares the same blood as me. I can safely say I have family in the UK.

I am going about my business on this particular day. I have a day off and I go to the town centre for some shopping. I am going about doing what I am doing when suddenly I hear, 'maJele'. Someone is calling me. I turn around, and there is Nomusa standing in front of me. We embrace, kiss and hug and look at each other in disbelief. We last saw each other years ago in Zimbabwe. We sit down and have a brief catch up. We go down memory lane, college years, assignments. It turns out we have both been in the UK for more or less the same amount of time. We exchange contacts and get close again. We do stuff together, cry and laugh together. We have a beautiful friendship.

I have managed to get an interview that will place me in a senior role within a care home. I'm told the job is mine if I want it. My passport comes back from the Home Office and I have been granted a two-year visa.

No words can describe the pain of being separated from my family, especially my children. I cry myself to sleep most nights. The only thing that keeps me going is hope. A hope that surely this cannot go on forever, a hope that one day this will pass. The worst times are on their birthdays. I'm not around to hug or kiss them. I am now a voice over the phone.

Tomorrow will be Mother's Day, and I am sitting in church. The children's department has organised something special for mothers. All mothers are asked to stand so I also stand. I am a mother, right? I'm not sure if I should stand or not. I stand up anyway.

The children come out from the lower youth hall into the main church building and each searches for their beautiful mama, they spot them, go straight to them and hand them a gift. I watch them as they walk past. They hug, kiss and hand over tokens of appreciation. I am still standing, hoping I will also be recognised as a mother. After all, mothers were asked to stand. Is it presumptuous of me to stand?

By now I am fighting back the tears. I have children, and I am a loving mother. I watch the mothers' reactions as they receive their gifts. How I pray for someone to come over and wrap their arms around me. Realising this is not going to happen, in shame I sit myself down. My head is down for the rest of the service, tears as my companion. My heart aches even more for my children. I want to hold them, to smell them and to look into their eyes as they tell me they love me. Is that too much to ask? Tears continue to roll.

After the service I don't linger around to mingle and to greet. I head straight home. The afternoon is spent in tears, crying my heart out.

There are times when I have resentment towards those that have their children with them and around them. It makes me feel guilty and irresponsible. What sort of a mother abandons her children? In my case, a loving caring one? My daily prayer begs God to take away the guilt and keep my children under his wings. Right now, that is more than I can do for them, fully commit them to God.

The situation is not getting any better in Zimbabwe. Individual and group prayers are said on behalf of that beloved country. If only God can remove the government of the day. We survive on hope. Life is managed through phone calls. I am not sure if I will ever see my children alive again, but one thing is for sure: they are being well looked after. I have all confidence in my little sister, and my parents also do the best they can for my children.

Before I can blink one year is gone, then the next and the next. I work every hour God sends. Life is a routine. Work, home, sleep and thank God for Sabbath. I meet friends, laugh, have lunch and its good, and then it's back to work, and a day off is unwelcome because it means no pay. Sabbath rest is enough.

My two-year visa will be expiring soon. My manager approaches me and informs me the company wants to sponsor me for a work permit at the end of my visa. I am over the moon. The necessary paperwork is put together and I will be personally going to the Home Office.

I convince myself there is no need for me to seek asylum in the UK. This is going to sound silly but trust me,

Reader, the thought of having to tell my life story to some stranger, who most probably won't relate to me, was not at all attractive. The words 'asylum' and 'refugee' have become associated with so much negativity. Some of the indigenous population see us as not deserving to be in their country, and maybe they are justified. Some even question the truth of our stories. You see, Reader, in my opinion being a political refugee does not strip me of any dignity and respect. With all these pressures around me, getting sponsorship is heaven-sent.

Home Office – Part 1

'When we were children, we used to think that when we were all grown-up we would no longer be vulnerable. But to grow up is to accept vulnerability... To be alive is to be vulnerable
Madeleine L'Engle

I prepare for the trip to the Home Office. All my documentation is in place and neatly put away in a file. I am going to the Home Office, so being organised is important.

Tuesday morning and I am there before opening time. Already there is a long queue. There is something about that building. Somehow it reminds you that you are not from here, you are a foreigner. Nonetheless, I stay put.

I go in and I am attended by a young, beautiful black lady. She is definitely younger than me, that I can tell. She takes my documents and does whatever she has to do. She scans them and then speaks to her colleague. I don't catch the gist of the conversation, but I know it's about my application. I am asked to proceed to the second floor of the building. This time a young man attends to me. He fills in a few forms, asks a few questions and takes my payment. He tells me I will need to come back in a month's time to collect my passport. He gives me an appointment, and I head back home.

Weeks roll by and it's time to go back and collect my

passport. I am a handed a ticket and directed straight to the same young man who attended to me a month ago. He still remembers me, *oh that's a good thing*. He tells me to wait. I wait for an hour before he calls me over to his booth.

He beckons me over but this time he directs me to go through a door next to his booth. Well, maybe because I'm getting my sponsorship visa I have to go to another office or something. He smiles at me and I smile back as I go through the door.

They are two police officers waiting.

'I am charging you with . . . false instrument . . . anything you say or . . . may be used . . .' By now I am in a spin. *What is going on here? Did I just hear correctly, are these officers talking to me or what? I must be having a funny turn.*

'Do you understand what I have just said?'

'No,' I answer back. That is God's honest truth. I do not understand what is happening or what the police officer is saying.

'OK. We will explain everything at the police station,' the second officer answers.

'Did you just say police station?' I ask.

'Yes, because you have just been arrested.'

'Arrested for what?' I am physically sick, I mean I vomit and miss one of the officer's shoes by an inch.

They bundle me into their car and take me to what I soon find out is Croydon police station. The same recital about not having to say anything continues. I am in a daze and my head is spinning. Another violent sickness. This time I have three bouts of it. Medical personnel are sent to attend to me and I'm offered some anti-sickness medication. Once I'm calm the nightmare continues.

How does this thing work and since when has collecting

a passport led to an arrest? Suddenly there is talk of lawyers, and after humiliating strip searches I am put in a cell. Life has a way of landing you in places you never imagined. I would have thought you would have had more chance of finding me on the moon than in a police cell, yet here I am, in a stinking cell.

A wise person once said to me, 'You don't necessarily have to go out and look for trouble, trouble comes looking for you.' This is trouble I have definitely not invited. It comes knocking at my door and invites itself in. I can't tell you much about that afternoon, only that it is spent in a dirty stinking cell with tears for companionship.

Around 4 p.m. a lawyer comes to see me and attempts to unravel this nightmare. It transpires the two-year visa on my passport is not authentic.

Finally, I am released to go home. The next nine months are spent attending appointments with lawyers in attempts to prove my innocence. I lose about a stone and a half in weight. I am worried and fearful. People think I must be on some exercise or healthy living plan. *I am in hell*; I feel like shouting it at them. The few trusted friends with whom I share this do their best to encourage, support and keep my spirits up. As is human nature, some believe me and others don't. Not a word to my family back home. This will be too much for them to deal with. We protect those we love, and I'm no different.

Trial Day

And once the storm is over, you won't remember how you made it through, how you managed to survive. You won't even be sure, whether the storm is really over. But one thing is certain. When you come out of the storm, you won't be the same person who walked in. That's what this storm's all about.
Haruki Murakami

I have prayed and fasted and done all that is humanly possible. Deep in my heart I know I am innocent. What else can I do?

A few friends come together this particular Saturday night and we hold an all-night prayer vigil. They encircle me and pray for me. When everyone has prayed, one of the ladies speaks. This is what she says: 'As I was praying I saw a lion standing next to you. The lion was calm and looked as though it was watching over you.' I don't know how to react to this, So I don't. I let it pass.

We move to a singing session. I am sitting at the end of the sofa and suddenly I can hear somebody else's voice. It's as though there is someone singing next to me. I am confused. The voice is coming from somewhere. The voice is distinct. I turn to look so I can see where this voice is coming from. There is definitely no one sitting next to me. This is puzzling.

It's two days before my trial and I have a strange dream.

More often than not I forget my dreams the minute I open my eyes in the morning, but I remember this one. In this dream, I am in a room with a few girlfriends and we are sleeping. The dream is set in my boarding school dormitory. We settle to sleep. I feel I have a cramp in both my legs. So I stretch in an effort to relieve the cramp. As I am stretching my legs I feel something warm and fluffy on my feet. When I look, I see a big, golden brown lion. In fear I attempt to move my legs away so I don't startle the lion.

The dream troubles me. What's with all these lions and me? Well I don't know and whatever will be, let it be, I tell myself.

The trial day is finally here and I am on my way to Croydon Crown Court. Before I leave home I say a prayer, 'Lord, let me say only what I need to say. Let me not attempt to fight and prove my innocence the way I think I should.'

As I sit in the dock I cast a quick glance at the members of the jury now taking their seats. *Well, my fate is in the hands of these men and women.* The court is in session. I'm asked to stand and confirm my name and my place of abode. The presiding judge is a lady. She shows a fascination at the way my second name is pronounced. She attempts to pronounce it and she sends the court room occupants into fits of laughter. For about two minutes I try to teach her how to pronounce it. In my head I am thinking, *Don't lure me into a false sense of security here, lady. Get on with the business of the day.*

The first witness is a representative from the Home Office. Guess who? The young lady who first attended to me on my first visit. Her witness statement included an allegation that I had had concerns over the visa stamp in my passport and had asked if I could have it verified.

I am sitting in the dock, and by now I am shaking my head. *Why is this woman telling lies to the court? She is under oath, for goodness' sake. Well, that's it for me. I am done. Prison here I come.*

The defence questions her and she continues in her tirade to discredit me. There appears to be communication between the prosecution team and the defence team. The prosecution asks the judge to grant a recess and the judge announces that we have to adjourn. I'm not sure who says what.

I find myself a little seat in the canteen. Everybody is buying coffee and sandwiches like there is no tomorrow. I spot my lawyer and the defence lawyer having a deep discussion while sipping their strong coffee. How I wish I could be part of the discussion so I could tell the prosecution lawyer his first witness just lied under oath.

My lawyer comes over to me and proposes I get something to eat. *Really?* If the idea of having vomit over her legal robes is exciting then maybe, but otherwise food is the least of my worries right now.

So the next time you are tempted to say you are starving, please think again. Starvation is when going without food is not a choice but a reality.

Recess is over and it's back to the court room. Soon it will be my turn to be quizzed. My palms are sweating at the prospect and I am scared out of my wits.

'Due to the revelations from the witness that the accused actually approached the Home Office showing concern over the visa stamp on her passport, the prosecution has concluded the case against the accused is to be dropped and the accused is acquitted. It is clear that the accused did not seek to deceive nor did she seek to get a visa through fraudulent means as stated by the Home Office,' the judge announces.

Maybe this time I have truly not understood: after all, English is not my first language but my third. My lawyer throws a glance and smiles at me. I don't reciprocate her smile, I'm scared. I need to be sure I heard the judge correctly.

'Out of interest, has the jury reached a decision?' the judge asks and she appears to be laughing as she poses the question.

'Yes we have, Your Honour.'

'You may read the verdict.'

'We find the defendant not guilty.'

My defence lawyer turns around again and looks at me. She gives me the thumbs up. Confident this time, I gesture back. From that moment on all I remember is the judge ordering the Home Office officials to hand over all of my documents in their possession.

'Hope things work out for you.' My lawyer smiles as we say our goodbyes.

As I make my way to the train station everything falls into place. The lions: who is the great Lion of Judah? Jesus. His divine self was in the courtroom and He has just roared on behalf of His child and vindicated me. Be cynical all you want over this, it's OK and I will not hold it against you. I am also a cynic over many issues, concepts and believes, so nothing gives me the right to expect you to make sense of what I am saying right now. The truth still remains. Again something else is put into perspective; the prayer I said in the morning was answered. The only thing I had to say in that court room was my name.

You would be expecting me to be champing at the bit with joy. It's only now that the weight of the lifted burden takes its toll. Only now do I realise how heavy this burden had rested on my weak shoulders. My feet are heavy and my heart is struggling to keep in rhythm with the rest of my body. My body and mind are struggling to come to terms with the events of the last hour or so. The journey from the court room to the station should only take at least ten minutes but it takes way more than that. I can tell that my feet and my mind are not in sync. I feel faint and nauseous. I am convinced some passers-by might conclude I am suffering the effects of alcohol or drugs. *What just happened in that court room? Can someone please give me a good old mama's pinch so I can rise from this slumber?*

A few minutes away from the train station I spot the five Home Office officials that were in court for my case. The court is not far away from the Croydon Home Office building. Tails between their legs, they walk along, I presume going back to work. If their looks could kill, then let me drop dead. Two of them approach me.

'We need your passport back,' one of them says. 'The judge was wrong to order us to give it back to you.'

My blood boils. *Am I not in a western, civilised country which prides itself on upholding the law to the letter? Since when does it believe in kangaroo courts that spring up anywhere a good old Mopani tree provides wall-to-wall shade? Let's just give the judge the benefit of the doubt here, I know I should not be approached on the street in this manner.*

By now all five of them have surrounded me. This is intimidation and none of them is intimidating me, no way. I look each of them in the eyes, one at a time. 'Go and tell that to the judge. If you think I am handing my passport over to you then I suggest you think again. If you will excuse me please, I have a journey ahead of me.'

Have I just challenged five Home Officers in the middle of the street? Oh dear. I push past, almost sweeping one of them to the ground. After taking a few steps I turn round and they are still staring at me. The lady who testified and one of the male officers make rude hand gestures. I ignore them and continue with my journey. I find myself a seat in the train. My mind, body and soul are shattered to the very core. The last nine months have been a challenge. My body is light. My eyes close and I fall into a deep sleep. The next time I open my eyes I am at Luton train station.

As I turn my phone on, there are countless messages from worried friends. I find strength to respond to one of them and ask her to pass on the good news to others.

Croydon One Last Time

And I said to the man who stood at the gate of the year:
'Give me a light that I may tread safely into the
unknown'. And he replied: 'Go out into the darkness and
put your hand into the hand of God. That shall be to you
better than light and safer than a known way.
Minnie Louise Haskins

Zimbabwe continues to be in meltdown. Now it's time to face reality once and for all and accept and declare the truth: I am a refugee in the UK. I am constantly watching the news on the TV. What is going on back home is heartbreaking. People's homes are being demolished; the political unrest beggars belief. People are broken. It is utter mayhem.

Unfortunately, the journey to that much-needed freedom has to start back at the Croydon Home Office. I already have history with that place and if the truth be told I would prefer to go somewhere different, but Croydon Home Office it is. Imagine if one of those nasty Home Office guys happens to be the one to attend to me. I'm sure they will have a field day.

The queue is long. I am given a ticket with a number, yes that's what I am for today: Number 319.

'Ticket number 319, please go to counter 15,' says a voice from the intercom. *Oh, that's me.* I locate counter 15 and move towards it. Privacy and dignity are non-existent today. The lady behind counter 15 has a loud voice, I mean really loud. Mine not so loud. I keep my voice low but loud enough for her ears. I don't want anyone who has nothing to do with my story to be part of it.

'Speak up,' she bellows from behind her desk. I try to raise my voice and throughout the interview she keeps bellowing I should speak up. The interview lasts about three hours. There are instances when she goes away for ages and I have to just sit and wait. Even a call of nature does not move me from that counter lest I am told that I have missed my opportunity. There is paperwork to sign, an ID card stating that I am an asylum seeker. She tells me that I will be receiving notification of another interview soon. I head back home and wait.

Solihull – The Big Interview

Be kind, for everyone you meet is fighting a harder battle.
Plato

Two weeks after the visit to Croydon I receive a letter informing me to attend another interview in Solihull. I make enquiries and plans on how to get there. Talk about a depressing building. It's grim; it shouts out: *Foreigner, immigrant, refugee, asylum seeker!* You name it, it says it all. Nothing about it is welcoming.

This is definitely a building designed for the unwelcome, those that come and 'take jobs' away from the indigenous, so they say. There is no evidence of any form of maintenance. Not one member of staff smiles. They all have straight faces. They speak with authority and are intimidating. Nature calls, and I move to the bathrooms to relieve myself, but my mind sends signals to my body and it switches off. Honestly, I cannot use those toilets. The toilets are so filthy. Wouldn't you expect such a public place to be maintained throughout the day, especially the toilets? Oh no, why maintain them for asylum seekers? *Where is our humanity, people?*

This is it, the big interview. This is make or break. It commences at 1 p.m. and lasts four hours. I am asked one hundred and eighty six questions all in all. Surely even anyone who is applying to go to the moon would not be asked so many questions.

After two months comes the response. My claim has been rejected. Talk about kicking a woman when she is already down in the gutter. It dawns on me; now I am officially a failed asylum seeker. Wait, somewhere in that rejection letter there is a paragraph mentioning I have the right to appeal. *Lord, there is still hope.* Now don't be fooled and think I took that in good faith. No. I am broken, I feel forgotten and forsaken. To go through with the appeal I need a lawyer, and they don't come cheap.

I am not looking at anything less than £1,000. There is no chance in heaven or hell of raising that kind of money. This is another game-over situation. I have nowhere to start. A good lawyer has been recommended to me. I make an appointment to see him anyhow, and true to my guess his fee is £1,000.

Girlfriends To the Rescue

*The fellowship of true friends who can hear you out,
share your joys, help carry your burdens, and correctly
counsel you is priceless.*
Ezra Taft Benson

It's a Friday evening and Val comes over so we can chat and really get to know each other. Women just love to chat. We put the world to rights, attempt to answer the question, whether there are still any good men around, and talk turns to food, fashion, shoes and handbags. We talk of life experiences. We cry, laugh and pray together, say goodbye and part. She has come up with a plan but says nothing to me. Having realised that I am probably not going to ask for the financial help that I so desperately need she spreads the word around to a few friends. By the end of the week, I put together what is in my little savings and what has been collected by friends and thank God, I have the money needed for the lawyer.

This experience teaches me another of life's lessons. Sometimes it is our own assumptions and prejudices that stop us from crying out for help. If you don't ask, people won't know you are in need. True, we all want to be private and keep our struggles to ourselves, but a genuine person never makes you feel you are indebted to them. However, this should also teach us not to take people for granted and take advantage of people's good nature. It is also not always possible for people to offer help at the time we need it. The emotional support goes a long way if that's what's available. I will forever be grateful to those who have reached out to me in so many ways.

The lawyer prepares his legal arguments and I prepare myself as well. I am going to tell it to the judge just as it is. No tricks, no gimmicks.

It's 14th of November 2008 and an immigration judge is hearing my grounds for appeal. The lawyer does his bit and the judge fires questions directly at me. There is a Home Office representative. Within about forty five minutes we are through.

'Who on earth was that woman I was representing today?' my lawyer asks as we leave the appeal centre.

'Pardon?'

'I don't know what was up with you but you were a different person in there.'

I don't give a response.

'Where did all that courage and those words come from?' he continues. I wish he would just shut up and drive his car. I am exhausted and in no mood for cheap talk right now.

I can't tell you what I'm supposed to have said or done in that appeal hearing. All I know is, I feel a peace and calmness. I have done what is humanly possible and now leave it all to God.

Finally There

'*If there is no struggle, there is no progress.*'
– Frederick Douglass

Exactly four weeks to the day after the appeal I receive some correspondence from the Home Office. Whatever the outcome, let it be well with my soul. It's a lengthy document, about six pages. Now I have been told by those who have walked this way before me that the crucial sentence to look for is the one which reads, *You have been granted refugee status under the Geneva convention.* Any other legal garbage really doesn't matter now.

There it is right at the end of the letter. I scream and jump; the floorboards squeak. After the jumping and screaming comes the wailing. I mean wailing. Have you seen African women at a funeral? You get the picture. Hands on my head I wail as though I have just been told someone close to me has died.

This journey has been long, lonely, dark and hard. Seven years, seven long years without my children. Seven hard years trying to survive, seven bleak years attempting to live a near-normal life. Seven years of an existence rather than living. For a good ten minutes I wail. It is hard to accept I am finally here.

Reader, whatever it is that you are going through shout out loud, 'And this too shall come to pass.' Weeping will endure, weeping has to endure. For some it's only for a season, for others more than two seasons and yet for others what appears a lifetime, your joy will come one morning, one day and one year. Hang in there; all is not lost.

After composing myself, there follows a prayer of thanks. I can't verbalise it as I want to. I say it with tears. God will understand my tears, so it's cool. I want God to hear my heart. A phone call to my sister follows. I feel her joy and love over the phone. Both overcome by emotion, we cry. The only thing she keeps saying to me is, 'You need to be with your children now, Sis, your children need you.'

I call a few close friends and tell them the good news.

Together at Last

Know from whence you came because if you know from whence you came, there is no limit to where you can go.
James Baldwin

MK drives to the airport. My belly feels funny. I don't know how I feel. I want to be excited and happy but realise that I am nervous. What if I fail to recognise them? What do they think of me as a mother and what if they are angry towards me? Do they really understand the sacrifice? All these questions scare me. I wish I had the answers to all my questions. I want the voice of reason to tell me all will be OK.

Nomusa and MK seem relaxed. The closer we get to the airport the more nervous I get. I feel pins and needles all over my body and my body starts to ache. A woman's instincts; Nomusa looks over towards me and reassures me. It's as though I'm having labour pains all over again. Suddenly it dawns on me, the experience I am about to go through is indeed a re-birth.

In silence I cope with the pain the best I know how. You would expect me to be jumping for joy. Sorry to disappoint: I'm not. I am dreading what I am about to deal with. I'm terrified. These are broken pieces, not even broken, but shattered. How does one put together shattered pieces? I don't know how to do that. I don't have a formula; not even Einstein can work this one out for me.

But I know someone who can mend at no charge, and makes everything perfect. That man, Reader, is my God. I only need to hand the pieces over.

'The plane has landed,' my brother says. I keep silent. Nomusa responds to him.

'They will be out any minute soon,' he speaks again.

I feel like shouting, 'Shut up!' to both of them. Nomusa senses my frustration and she puts her hand over my shoulder and asks if I am all right. Her touch irritates me even more. Out of courtesy I give her a nod. Many people come through. I peer through in an attempt to locate my babies.

From a distance I think I have spotted my son, or somebody who resembles him. Next to him is this gorgeous young girl clutching a big, cuddly teddy bear. She looks so cute. I keep looking, and the young girl looks like my daughter but I am not so sure. An air stewardess is walking along with them.

'There they are,' my brother says.

That is definitely my daughter. She has grown, she is a young lady. Guess what, Reader, in my head I am still looking for the little seven-year-old girl I left behind! Unfortunately, she is not a little girl any more. I make an attempt to run towards them but my legs don't move, my whole body freezes. I am like a statue.

The stewardess brings them all the way to where I am standing. They have spotted me. I am still frozen and now I am crying. We hug, kiss and cry. I look up, hold my hands high and say, 'Thank you Lord.' Nothing really matters now. Nothing really counts. My little ones are here with Mummy, and that is all that matters.

The first night together. My daughter is fast asleep next to me. I wake up, put the light on and watch her as she is peacefully sleeping. I admire her for about thirty minutes, and pull the covers up to cover her arm.

One thing is for sure, they have been well taken care of. God provided my sister and gave her this love so she could share it with them. She has looked after them as her own. Imagine, friends, for the entire seven years, I never once received a phone call to say they are not well, or they are in hospital or they have been involved in an accident or something of that nature. Now tell me, if that isn't God, then who?

I have friends and acquaintances whose children have died back in Zimbabwe. Some have received calls to say their children have been rushed to hospital. Does that mean my sister was Super Aunty? Not at all; it means God has been overly gracious to me. The question is, how do I repay my sister for the sacrifice? The truth is, no matter what I do, I will never get close.

Embrace your family and be there for them whenever you can. Be the glue that holds your family together. The grand reunion on the 16th of October 2009 goes into my box of memories along with many others.

I may never make up for lost time, never make up for missed birthdays, never make up for missed parent evenings and many such events, but one thing is for sure: I will endeavour to enjoy the moments from now on. For now is the moment granted to me. We have this moment to cherish and love each other.

So Near And Yet So Far

*Don't let today's disappointments cast a shadow on
tomorrow's dreams.*
Unknown Author

My five-year refugee visa has restrictions, and rightfully
so. I can travel anywhere in the world apart from
Zimbabwe. The five years have rolled by, and I am now
eligible to apply for British Citizenship. I will put all the
paperwork in on time and all will be well.

Finally, I can almost smell the home soil. Very soon I
will be locking hands with and hugging loved ones of long
ago. To say I am excited is underplaying the whole thing. I
truly don't know how I feel but one thing is for sure, I will
be going home. I picture my beloved Mama, I picture my
doting dad and the world's greatest sister. Oh how great
that moment will be!

I picture myself standing in Mama's kitchen watching
her cook up a scrumptious meal, and I can also see Dad
stealing a look towards me as though to say, 'Is this really
my daughter?' I can almost hear him heave a sigh of relief
and shed a tear or two in delight at the imminent return of
his big girl. I can see the wall-to-wall smile on my sister's
face. She is lost for words, and looks on as though she is
dreaming. She attempts to pinch me. I have all these
pictures in my head.

I remember the guava tree, the one we where would not

dare get the fruits unless on Mama's say so. The guava tree, a favourite place for Dad to sit underneath and get shade from the scorching African sun. How I'm going to enjoy sitting next to him and listening to his funny stories, some of which I doubt are true. He will tell me more of his growing up stories in Zambia, and how he belongs to the chieftainship clan. How I'm going to laugh and make fun of him. I can see Mama casting a glance at us and shaking her head.

It's been fourteen years since I last saw my parents, my sister, my eldest brother and the extended family.

'Hang in there, Dad, I'm coming home this year,' I tell my dad in one of our telephone conversations. He hasn't been well, and I guess I'm trying to cheer him up. His voice changes, suddenly I can feel it pick up and he answers in great anticipation. That is the honest truth, I'm going home and I will see him.

Its early morning on 15th of March. It's Mother's Day in the UK. Soon mothers will be spoiled rotten with burnt toast, scrambled eggs and baked beans. I giggle. I know their little ones will spoil them. I'm still in my bed, though wide awake. My phone rings and my parents' number comes up on my phone. This is definitely not good. By now my hands are shaking, I'm not sure if I should pick up the phone or not. When I pick it up I don't speak. I wait for whoever is on the other end of the phone to say something.

'*Na Kenny ubaba kasekho.*' (Dad is gone). That is Mama's voice. In the background I can hear my sister crying. I am mumbling words and I don't know what I am saying.

I pace up and down, talk to myself and cry. *This is not fair. I promised Dad I would be coming home to see him; why did he not hang in there? If he has waited for fourteen years, surely what's a few months?* I am distraught, I want my daddy. I am mad at God. I feel shortchanged here. I just wanted to see my dad, to talk to him one last time, was that really too much to ask?

Guilt takes over. *Maybe if I had been home, Dad would have lingered on for as long as we wanted him to. Why, Lord? I have been asking you to grant us life till we meet again under the sun. Why couldn't God just grant me this request?* Sadness fills my heart. I don't know how long I grapple with God. I feel hard done by. *Only a few months, then I would have seen both my parents.*

No woman or man is an island unto themselves. Soon I realise I need that human contact to ride on this journey with me. I spread the word to family and friends in the UK, and true to humanity, once again people don't fail. There is a constant stream of words of comfort, and for that I am eternally grateful.

In the midst of all this heartache, I am reminded that life is not promised to any of us. Death, unfortunately is certain. I realise that goodbyes do matter. Never in a million years would I have known that that goodbye and that embrace fourteen years back was the final goodbye.

Reader, make your goodbyes count. When you get up in the morning before leaving home, give your nearest and dearest a heartfelt goodbye. Let them know how much you love them. Part with loved ones on a happy note, yes even that wayward teenager, and yes that toddler who is always throwing tantrums. Life is not guaranteed. We like to think we are in control, but the honest truth is, we are not. There is a higher power in control. *Until then, rest in peace, Dad.*

So What's The Big Deal?

I am not what happened to me, I am what I choose to become.
C.G. Jung

The question could be asked, so what is the big deal? Life bruises, it leaves one aching emotionally and physically. Tears and hurt, a part of life we would rather do without. Life consists of disappointments, weathering ferocious storms with seemingly no hope of coming through the other side.

Life, it makes us bitter, it compels us to seek that 'sweet revenge'. Our life has more bitter, painful experiences rather than joyous ones. Such is our life.

Most of the time it feels like we are all alone against the world. We cannot see any way out of its misery. Experience teaches wisdom, the greatest tragedy would be the failure to learn from the experiences.

I have a choice, and I want to choose wisely. I can choose for my experiences to define who I become. I can choose to be bitter and angry, or I can choose to become a better person, not only for myself but for others around me. I can choose to rise up, dust off and continue in the race, for if the truth be told, ahead lies many more storms to be endured.

Today I make a lasting choice. I choose to endeavour to smile even if I don't feel like it. I choose to tell others I'm here if they need me, to reach out, to listen and not be judgemental. Today I allow God to shape me into the diamond He would have me be, rather than the one I think I ought to be.

Reader, if God can work with me, and give me the strength to rise up again, you too can still rise above that which is chaining you.

This is the story of my life so far, what is your story? Is it one filled with failures and regrets? Is it one full of 'once upon a time' themes? Could your story be one you are ashamed of, not willing to share because it is wriggled with hurts, confusion, failed dreams, and deep-seated pain that has left you with scars? Maybe your story is one filled with triumphs, love and untold success. Whatever the story of your life is, will you allow God to rewrite it?

There is no greater agony than bearing an untold story inside of you.
Maya Angelou

Regina Jele-Ncube

Acknowledgments

Mama: The greatest teacher there ever will be. I owe it all to you. You are indescribable, priceless and I will always be indebted to you. You picked me up, cleaned my wounds, soothed my soul, and loved me even more. Mama, I love you.

Dad: You plodded along and played your part. I wish I could turn back the hands of time. I'm proud to say I am Daddy's girl. Until Jesus returns, rest in peace, Baba.

Patricia: The world's greatest sister! There will never be another you. I dare the world to show me another you. You have been my confidante, my best friend, my right-hand woman. You never judged me. You listened and gave sound advice. You worked hard, sacrificed, gave up your dreams. Nonks and Kenny wouldn't be who they are had it not been for your love and sacrifice. PJ, you are my world. I love you to the moon and back, Little Sis.

MK & Shacky: Every girl needs brothers in her life. MK, your quiet nature has been like medicine to my soul. Shacky, you have always respected me as your little sister and when I have allowed you, you were willing to play your big brother role. I love you guys.

Agrippa: To the memory of a dear, departed brother. He sleeps awaiting the return of our Lord Jesus.

The Jarretts: You not only opened your home to me but you opened your hearts and let me in. My adopted mum and dad in the UK.

Linda Chisese: Well, where do I start, thank you for letting me mother you. Many a night we spent in prayer. We cried and laughed. I hope I have managed to positively influence your life. I am so proud of the mother you have become. Remember that even at my best I am still a flawed human.

Hilda Wilson: Hey, girlfriend. Thank you.

Luton Central SDA Church Members: Well, where do I start? The many prayers and the support rendered. The encouragements, words of comfort, hugs, kisses, the tissues to dry the tears, the shoulders you allowed me to lean on. Words cannot explain. You held me together. Let us continue to hold on. Our heavenly home is but at hand.

To the many friends/acquaintances/colleagues: I have made so many. You have wiped a tear, shared words of comfort, listened as I poured my heart out, some of you waking up in the wee hours of the morning to pray with me. I cannot attempt to list the names of all the people that have touched my life, for to do so is to run the risk of omitting others. To all of you – may God richly bless you now and always.

More Books by Regina Jele-Ncube

Poetry
Deep Within My Soul

Children's Fiction
Thandi – Origins, Differences & Friendships

Lightning Source UK Ltd.
Milton Keynes UK
UKOW01f0655090517

300789UK00001B/21/P